THE
AFRICAN
Baobab

THE
AFRICAN
Baobab

RUPERT WATSON

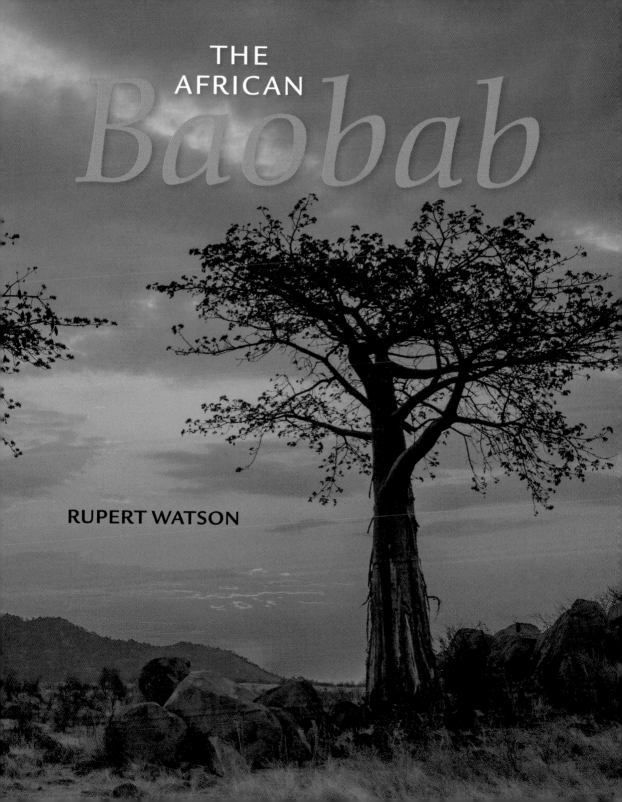

Published by Struik Nature
(an imprint of Penguin Random House
South Africa (Pty) Ltd)
Reg. No. 1953/000441/07
The Estuaries No. 4, Oxbow Crescent,
Century Avenue, Century City, 7441
PO Box 1144, Cape Town, 8000 South Africa

Visit www.struiknature.co.za and join the Struik Nature
Club for updates, news, events and special offers.

First published in 2007
Second edition 2024

10 9 8 7 6 5 4 3 2 1

Publisher: Pippa Parker
Managing editor: Roelien Theron
Editor: Natalie Bell
Concept designer: Dominic Robson
Designer: Emily Vosloo
Cartographer: James Whitelaw
Picture researcher: Colette Stott
Proofreader: Helen de Villiers

Reproduction by Studio Repro
Printed and bound in China by Toppan Leefung
Packaging and Printing (Dongguan) Co., Ltd.

MIX
Paper from
responsible sources
FSC® C104723

ISBN 978 1 77584 869 1 (Print)
ISBN 978 177584 870 7 (ePub)

Front cover: Sunrise at Baines' Baobabs campsite –
AdobeStock
Half-title page: White baobab flower, Senegal, rainy
season – AdobeStock
Title page: Sunset and baobabs, Ruaha National Park,
Tanzania – AdobeStock
Imprint page, left: Old baobab flower; **right:** Laminae
Contents page, left: Digitate leaf; **right:** Giraffe feeding
Spine: Baobab fruit (vector image) – AdobeStock
Back cover: Many of the baobabs on Lekhubu Island in
Botswana defy thoughts on how trees should be shaped.
Back cover, author photograph: Mary Ann Burris

Contents

Bu hobab

Baobab trees are living monuments,
the oldest natural things in Africa,
outlasting every plant and animal
around them. These trees have
evolved formidable resilience in
order to survive in some of the driest,
rockiest areas of this continent. Yet,
for all the hostility of much of their
habitat, African baobabs live longer
and grow larger than most other trees
in the world. That is the great paradox
of their existence.

The name 'baobab' is most likely a corruption of
bu hobab, roughly translated from 16th century Arabic
to mean 'having many seeds'. From one such seed
grew the Sagole Baobab in South Africa, presently the
largest of its kind in the world.

THE AFRICAN BAOBAB

BU HOBAB

Solitary trees

Trees as huge as baobabs would seem to belong in forests. There, trees grow branch to branch, nourished by their decaying leaves, collectively protecting each other from the forces of wind and storm, and providing shade, shelter and succour for new saplings. Yet baobabs are usually solitary trees, shunning the mutual support system of the woodlands. They are also remarkably thirsty trees, and to satisfy that thirst they need space to stretch their roots so they can draw moisture into their huge, water-bloated trunks.

Sometimes baobabs do grow close to one another, almost close enough for branches to touch, and certainly for roots to meet and compete in their subterranean quest for liquid. These more closely grouped trees have all survived the random accidents of seed dispersal that brought them together, yet this still does not make them a community of trees. They survive despite – not because of – the nearness of their fellows.

Baobabs dotted the African savanna while our ancestors still lolloped around on four legs. The trees would have provided them with easily gathered fruit, while branches gave shelter from rain, sun and predators. As we gradually began to stand upright (perhaps some two million years ago), this freed up our hands to shape tools and may also have freed up our minds to start thinking 'how' and 'why' about the world. Early humans may have harvested honey

Baobabs essentially grow alone, often, like this one in Kenya's Tsavo West National Park, far from any others.

THE AFRICAN BAOBAB

from the bees' nests in these mighty trees, and appreciated the goodness in the leaves, even using hollow trees for their cave-like homes.

Probably not until much later, when *Homo* finally evolved into *erectus*, even *sapiens*, did we first entertain vague thoughts of greater, unseen forces outside this earthly realm. The world of primitive African people spread as far as their furthest travels. The biggest thing that moved in it was the elephant, and the biggest living thing that didn't was the baobab. The trees were as near to permanent as any living thing could be. If any plant or animal were to inspire notions of animism or religion, and to offer resting places for spirits or gods, surely it would be the baobab.

The baobab in mythology

While early animistic credos imbued baobabs with spirits of their own, a belief in a god was probably necessary to make sense of the provenance of these spectral behemoths.

In most myths of baobab creation, the tree is seen to be standing on its head, roots in the air – the ultimate 'upside-down tree'. A popular legend has it that one of the first trees God created was the baobab. When it saw the next tree, a slender palm, the baobab started grumbling that it should be taller. God heeded the baobab's complaint, but no sooner had the tree grown to reach the palm's tops, than it began to covet the flame tree's spectacular flowers. But when it, too, produced flowers, this was still not enough for the baobab. Next, it moaned that, unlike the fig, it had no fruit. This was too much, even for God, and in a rage, he wrenched the baobab out of the ground and dashed it back in, head first.

The Giriama on the Kenyan coast have a different story to tell. They say that the sweltering devil lay down to rest in the shade of a baobab tree. Enraged to find it leafless, as the tree is for nearly two-thirds of the year, the devil tore it out of the ground and replanted it upside down. Further south, the San of southern Africa dance the story of the baobab's creation by the Great Spirit, who,

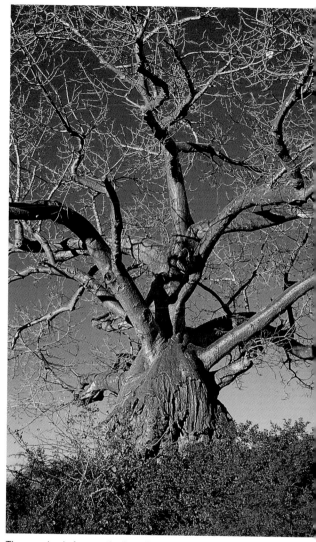

The species is frequently described as growing with its roots in the air, hence the epithet 'upside-down trees'. David Livingstone thought these trees resembled upturned carrots.

according to their folklore, gave a different species of tree to every animal. The last at this great arboreal distribution was the hyaena, who was so dissatisfied at being handed the baobab that it slammed the tree into the ground upside down.

The scientific theories regarding the baobab's emergence on Earth are much more prosaic, and almost as speculative. Pachyderms of the plant kingdom – like some of the great thick-skinned mammals still living around them – baobabs look like forgotten relics of a former age. It takes no great leap of imagination to visualize dinosaurs rubbing their wrinkled hides along the equally wrinkled bark of the trees, although, in fact, true dinosaurs were long gone from this planet by the time baobabs evolved into anything like the tree we recognize today.

With a baobab generation spanning well over 100 years, perhaps much more, the tree's response to environmental shifts is inevitably far more leisurely than that of shorter-lived plants. Yet, while the march of change may have been slow, the genus *Adansonia* has not halted in its evolutionary tracks, like coelacanths, hagfish and cycads have done. In addition to *Adansonia digitata* (the baobab of Africa and of this book), botanists currently recognize seven other well-described species: one in Australia and six in that living laboratory of evolution, Madagascar.

Taxonomically speaking, the genus *Adansonia* rested within the Bombacaceae family until recently.

Small by plant standards, this family's boundaries were ill-defined, and its members have now been clumped back into the enormous family of Malvaceae, which contains among its 4,200 species such diverse plants as hibiscus, durian, cotton, cocoa and linden trees. Still, no matter in which family the baobabs sit, their closest relatives remain those trees in the genus *Ceiba* (once *Chorisia*), whose flagbearers are the spectacular, pink-flowered, spiny-trunked bombax (*Ceiba speciosa*) and the kapok (*C. pentandra*), which, like the African baobab, is also pollinated by bats.

The baobabs of Madagascar

With so many different endemic baobabs, the island of Madagascar must be where the common ancestor gradually diversified. The ancestral seed pod probably arrived from the African mainland, providing the raw original for the subsequent evolution of the six species we recognize today.

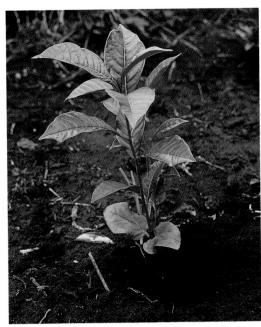

The striking pink flower of the closely related spiny-trunked bombax, whose pods open up on the tree before wind then disperses the seeds.

It is difficult to recognize young baobab trees because their leaf configuration differs from that of mature trees.

THE AFRICAN BAOBAB

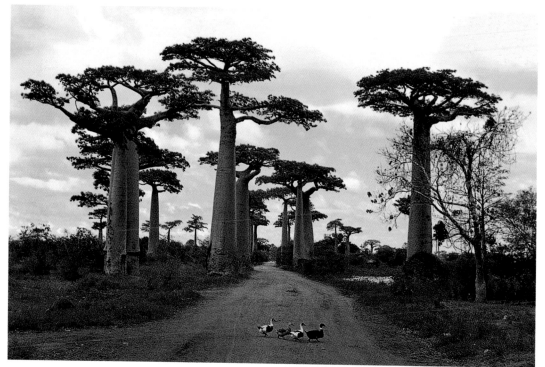

Above: Perhaps the most photographed baobabs in the world, Madagascar's *Adansonia grandidieri* on the road to Kirindy Mitea National Park. Right: *Adansonia perrieri* and *A. rubrostipa* are two *Adansonia* species that are indigenous to Madagascar.

All are sufficiently closely related to belong to the genus *Adansonia*, and are distinguished by differences in trunk size, leaf shape and flower colour.

The lofty *Adansonia grandidieri* and *A. suarezensis* are grouped together into a subgenus, distinguished from the others by, among other things, large seeds, winter flowering, classic flat-topped crowns, and thin-shelled pods, which usually break open when they hit the ground.

The other four Malagasy species, *A. perrieri*, *A. madagascariensis*, *A. za* and *A. rubrostipa*, are characterized, along with micro-differences in the shapes and colours of their exquisite flowers, by blooming in summer and having pods with much thicker shells. Size and shape of trunk vary both

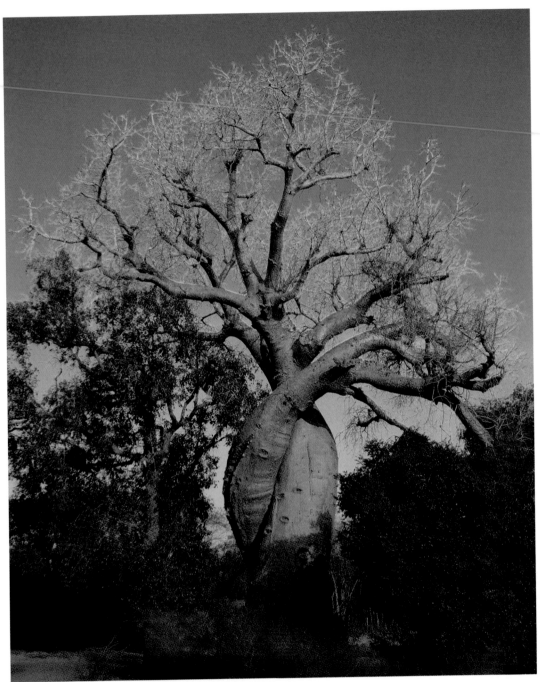

These entwined trunks of the 'Baobab Amoureux' near Kirindy are *Adansonia rubrostipa*.

THE AFRICAN BAOBAB

between and within species. Some are shorter, squatter trees with more of an African baobab look; others display the classical cylindrical figures of *A. grandidieri*, which is the most photographed of all the species in Madagascar. Those near Morondava, on the island's west coast, grace the covers of guidebooks, as well as the memories of visitors who have passed between them along the dirt road to Kirindy Mitea National Park. These same-sized trees, with cylindrical trunks, topped with tufts of horizontal branches, look as if they have been planted out along an avenue leading to a stately Malagasy home. They are, however, relicts of thick forest that has been slashed and burnt around them.

Closer to Kirindy, *A. rubrostipa* begins to replace *grandidieri* in a scrubby, less modified landscape. A few kilometres down a sandy sidetrack is the celebrated 'Baobab Amoureux' with its two trunks and entwining branches locked in a centuries-long embrace. Back to the main road and on towards the Park, scrub gives way to true forest and *A. za* is the dominant species. In early January, this most widespread of the Malagasy baobabs is in full, magnificent bloom, and fallen, yet still fragrant, yellow flowers cover the ground around the tree trunks, fine lines of red streaking the petals and stamens. And as if six species of baobab on a

single island were not enough, there are also populations of *A. digitata* on Madagascar's west coast, most likely introduced from Africa by settling humans rather than ocean currents. Being little known outside their native island, none of the Malagasy species is identified by any European sobriquet, other than the catch-all, 'baobab'. Local names tend not to distinguish between different species either, and *'renala'* ('mother of the forest') can refer to all the baobabs in a particular area, irrespective of species.

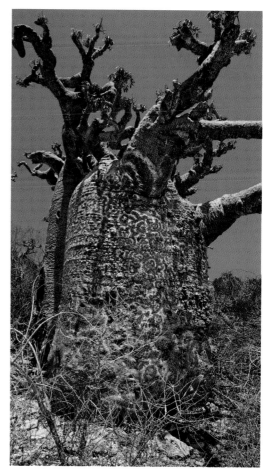

Adansonia rubrostipa is the smallest of the Madagascar baobabs and commonly called the fony baobab.

The classic five-fingered leaf that provides the African baobab with its species name, *digitata*.

The sun sets behind the soaring
pillars of the *Adansonia grandidieri*
on the Kirindy road, Madagascar.

The Australian boab

The northwest corner of Australia is home to the most intriguing member of *Adansonia* – at least in terms of how it got where it is. *A. gregorii* is stockier than its African relative, although still with a large enough girth for hollow specimens to have been used to incarcerate prisoners. This tree grows around the Kimberley region and the Victoria River, usually on rocky outcrops, and looks just as prehistoric in its barren Australian landscape as do the baobabs in Africa. The boab is particularly distinguished within the genus by sometimes growing in groups, as if the mother tree was raising young ones around her.

The 'boab', 'gouty-stemmed tree', 'bottle tree' or even 'dead rat tree' (referring to the pendulous fruit) was first brought to the attention of scientists in Europe by Allan Cunningham, on-board naturalist on HMC *Mermaid* during its survey of Australia's west coast between 1818 and 1822. Cunningham initially ascribed the boab to the genus *Capparis* (*C. gibbosa*), perhaps reluctant to believe there could possibly be baobabs in Australia. But once acknowledged as a baobab, it spent some years as *Adansonia gibbosa* (meaning 'swollen'), and although various authorities still use this name, the rules of taxonomic priority favour the original *gregorii*, so illuminating the name of AC Gregory, commander of the 1855 North Australia Exploring Expedition, but failing to describe anything about the tree.

Giant boab trees near Fitzroy Crossing in the Kimberley region of Western Australia.

THE AFRICAN BAOBAB

Baobab dispersal

With their nearest relatives far away in Madagascar and mainland Africa, the boabs beg an explanation for their presence in northwestern Australia. It is now commonly accepted that Africa, Madagascar, India, Antarctica and Australasia were all part of the great continuous landmass of Gondwanaland before its break-up around 140 million years ago. The simplest explanation for boabs being where they are today is that when the great slab of earth and rock that was Australia and Antarctica broke off and headed southwards, it carried away baobab ancestors, which eventually evolved into modern boabs. However, if baobabs existed before the break-up of Gondwanaland, they should be well spread throughout modern equatorial landmasses, and they are not. One would particularly expect to find them naturally distributed throughout India and the Arabian Peninsula. However, while a few baobabs are scattered across these areas, human beings, rather than continental drift, seem more likely to have deposited them there.

An alternative theory posits that millions of years after the break-up, seed pods floated across the ocean to the Australian subcontinent, which by then was more or less where it is now. This entailed pods bobbing thousands of miles over the water, to arrive eventually on a foreign shore receptive enough to enable a few seeds to germinate.

Both ideas strain the imagination. Because their wood contains so much water, and fallen baobabs decompose so quickly, the trees are poor fossilizers. The dates of the oldest African fossil records of other harder-wooded baobab relatives suggest that the family was not around when Gondwanaland began separating. This adds support to the theory that seeds moved from one continent to another much later. So does the unlikelihood of baobabs surviving the lengthy period that Australia and Antarctica spent joined together, far south of the equator – a time during which a lot of the vegetation that the landmass had inherited from its ancestral connection to Africa was killed off by cold.

Boabs are distinguished from all other members of their genus by sometimes growing in family groups.

Therefore, bizarre though it may seem, the balance of evidence favours dispersal of baobab pods by sea from Africa to Madagascar and Australia. Malagasy baobabs are often found near rivers, suggesting their seeds are well adapted to water dispersal. Perhaps around 30 million years ago some ancestral baobab dropped pods into a river, which carried them out into the open ocean. Australia is a long journey away, even for a well-waterproofed baobab pod propelled by favourable winds and currents, and populating it with baobabs could have been at least a two-stage process. Pods may have first made landfall on islands en route, which are now submerged by higher water levels, with seeds from these new colonies finally making it to Australia.

Once there, a few more crucial metres remained to be covered, requiring almost as fortuitous a combination of events as the transoceanic odyssey. The contents of the pods had to get over the bare sand of the high-water mark into more receptive soils beyond. Earthquakes or volcanic eruptions cause exceptional waves. Tsunamis or other rogue waves – unique combinations of tides and winds – come rolling in to almost any coastline, providing that critical nudge inland that finally allows a seed to germinate on foreign soil. And if huge waves didn't send pods far inland, perhaps ancestral marsupials foraged along the beach, picking up exotic-looking seed packages before scampering off into the undergrowth to examine them in peace.

No two baobab silhouettes are remotely similar and each tree has a story to tell.

'Discovering' the baobab

The history of geographical exploration and the parallel expansion of the science of taxonomy brim with 'discoveries'. For the most part, 'discovery' is a euphemism for revealing to the western world places, plants and animals with which other humans have long been familiar. Yet only by collating the mass of these revelations was it possible to fit them into a grander design. Only when travellers ventured beyond their immediate horizons could plants and animals take their place in wider geographical or scientific contexts.

The first written reference to the tree that has become known as the baobab does not come from the pen of any European explorer, but from that of the scribe of the indefatigable traveller, Ibn Battuta, who was born in Tangier around 1304. After making his hajj to Mecca, he took to using Tangier as a base for journeys into India, down the coast of East Africa, as well as to Turkey and through the Middle East. It would be nearly 25 years before he returned to Tangier and, having done so, he was soon back on his camel, heading south, through the Sahara to Timbuktu and into the Niger basin.

More of a social historian than naturalist, Ibn Battuta's account of the interaction between Islam and animism is particularly fascinating. Still, naturalist or not, on his way to the Kingdom of Mali in 1353, he found:

'The road has many trees of great age and size; a caravan can shelter under
a single one of them. Some of them have no branches or leaves but the trunk
gives enough shade to shelter men. Some of these trees have rotted inside and
rainwater has collected there, as if it were a well. People drink this water.
In some of these trees are bees and honey, which people collect.'

THE AFRICAN BAOBAB

Ibn Battuta had been dead almost 100 years before Europeans, particularly the Portuguese with their long-established maritime traditions, began opening up the coast of Africa. Driven by the competitive urge to capture trade from Venetian traders, these early sailors launched their expeditions with aspirations of commercial empire-building rather than of exploring the natural world. Nonetheless, baobabs, growing so huge and often close to the sea, proved impossible to ignore.

In 1448, Gomes Eannes de Azurara, chronicling the exploration of Guinea-Bissau, writes of a certain tree as being 108 hands in circumference. It needs no name for us to guess its identity, nor does the one described some years later by the Venetian explorer, Alvise Ca' da Mosto (generally remembered as 'Cadamosto') during his second voyage down the West African coast. Having passed Cape Verde, he turned into the Gambia River, and a few miles upstream found the banks:

'... covered with numerous and very large trees which are everywhere throughout the country. Concerning the size of these, I may say that, at a spring near the river bank from which we drew water, there was a very great and broad tree; its height, however, was not in proportion to its size, for while we judged it to be about twenty paces high we found the girth by measurement to be about seventeen paces round the foot. It was hollow in many places, and its branches were very large so that they threw a deep shade around.'

Kunta Kinteh Island (formerly James Island) is in the middle of the Gambia River and renowned both for its baobabs and for the remnants of old colonial fortifications, which have earned it the status of a UNESCO World Heritage Site.

More observant travellers looked beyond the shapes and sizes of plants and animals to the ways in which the local people made use of them. As the Renaissance drew to a close, botanical research was largely motivated by the search for better drugs with which to treat wealthy Europeans. Prospero Alpini was an Italian herbalist and physician from Venice who spent three years in Cairo at the end of the sixteenth century, ostensibly acting as the private doctor to the Italian consul. The consul's health obviously held up well, because this sinecure seems to have given Alpini much spare time. This he devoted to botanical study, particularly of the sexual life of the date palm. His collected observations culminated in the publication of *De plantis Aegypti liber* (1592), which contained the first detailed written description of the baobab. Alpini had seen the fruit selling in the Cairo souks under the Arabic name *bu hobab*, which, roughly translated, means 'having many seeds'.

Baobab classification

As the tempo of overseas exploration increased, specimens of fauna and flora poured into nascent centres of research for analyzing and comparing, recording and naming, finding sameness and difference. To give this plethora of new information a semblance of order, a system of grouping and naming was vital. And so, taxonomy was born – first as an art, then a science, and now a biological necessity. The tradition of classification goes back to Aristotle, but not until John Ray catalogued over 18 000 different plants in *The Wisdom of God Manifested in the Works of Creation* (1691) were species first arranged in some sort of hierarchical order. As a clergyman, Ray's rigid belief in the biblical theory of Creation is not surprising, although later in life both he and his scientific successor, Carl Linnaeus, began to doubt the wisdom of denying any possibility of the emergence of new species. Ray defined the concept of a species and Linnaeus then developed the idea of classifying each one, using a binomial system of nomenclature focused on similarities between them.

Linnaeus did a lot of first-hand research in his native Sweden. For specimens and descriptions from elsewhere in the world he relied upon submissions from observant travellers. One of these was Michel Adanson – a French naturalist, small in stature, with vast energy, a huge head and masses of red hair. By dint of contacts and enthusiasm, Adanson had found himself a four-year posting with

These Senegal baobabs are growing unusually close together and have had their branches lopped off so the leaves can be fed to livestock.

THE AFRICAN BAOBAB

the *Compagnie de L'Occident et des Indes*, arriving on the West Africa coastline in 1749 to research the natural resources of what is now Senegal.

Adanson's reaction on first seeing a baobab shows how unprepared he was for this botanical bombshell. In his *Histoire naturelle du Senegal* (1757), published in Paris and translated by 'an English Gentleman' two years later, he relates:

'They carried me to a particular spot where I saw a herd of antilopes; but I laid a-side all thoughts of sport, as soon as I perceived a tree of a prodigious thickness, which drew my whole attention. This was a calabash-tree, which the Jaloffes call goui in their language. There was nothing extraordinary in its height; for it was only about sixty feet: but its trunk was of a prodigious thickness.'

After measuring the branches, roots and trunks of other trees, he concluded that 'in short the whole of this calabash tree seemed to form a forest in itself'. And with these descriptions began the baobab's remarkably brief and, by the standards of the time, uncontroversial, introduction to modern science. Before returning from his African travels in 1754, Adanson was able to send an account of the baobab to his mentor in France, Bernard Jussieu, who had created the Trianon Gardens for Louis XV. This account in turn found its way to Linnaeus in Sweden in time for inclusion in *Species Plantarum*, published while Adanson was still in Africa.

Linnaeus had first propounded his binomial system of classification in *Systema Naturae* in 1735, and there can be no greater testimony to its logical

MICHEL ADANSON
(Botaniste)
Membre de l'Académie des Sciences,
Né à Aix (B. du Rhône) le 7 Avril 1727,
Mort à Paris le 3 Aoust 1806.

Michel Adanson, the French botanist after whom the genus takes its name.

efficacy than that it still endures today. With the first of Madagascar's endemic baobabs only to be scientifically described some 150 years later, the African tree clearly needed its own genus. So, in the Frenchman's absence, and encouraged by Jussieu, Linnaeus chose to Latinize 'Adanson' for the generic name, rather than Alpini or any of the many others who had earlier described the tree.

On his return to France, Adanson was overawed by the honour of finding his name incorporated into the formal description of the baobab. Having connected the tree with the fruit described by Alpini in the Cairo souk, he continued to advance 'baobab' as a more appropriate generic tag. Linnaeus was not to be deterred, and ultimately carved Adanson's name in the stone tablets of taxonomy by repeating the name *Adansonia digitata* in the 10th and definitive edition of *Systema Naturae* (1759).

Ironically, Adanson remained opposed to the Linnaean system of taxonomy. He spent much of his later working life trying to gather support for a massive 27-volume publication entitled *Universal Order of Nature*, which would have set him on a classification collision course with Linnaeus. Such encouragement as he received from his colleagues quickly evaporated in the heat of the French Revolution (1789–1799), during which Adanson lost almost everything but his head, his formidable mental energies finally deserting him in 1806. With the dying words 'Adieu, immortality is not of this world', he requested that one flower from each of the 58 botanical families he had categorized according to his own formula be placed on his coffin. However, immortality *has* shown itself to be of this world, at least in so far as his name lives on in the taxonomy of trees. *Adansonia digitata* remains the African baobab's Latin name, finding its place in the list of around 400 000 species of plants on Earth, and has had to withstand very little serious attempt to change it. *Adansonia bahobab* and *Baobabus digitata* were both half-heartedly floated as more acceptable alternatives, but too late to overturn the name Linnaeus had over 260 years earlier ascribed to the tree.

There are as many local African words for 'baobab' as there are languages spoken where the trees grow – and a lot more besides, because some tribes make even finer distinctions between trees of the same species. The authors of the great compendium of ethnobotanical knowledge, *The Medicinal and Poisonous Plants of Southern and Eastern Africa*, included 68 vernacular names, and there are probably just as many others missing from the list. Particularly striking is the fact that at least a quarter of the words on the list are variations on the *mbuyu* or *muyu* theme, showing the linguistic links between the present-day fragments of the great Bantu diaspora. In Swahili, the lingua franca of East Africa, baobab is *mbuyu*, and this echoes down Tanzania in the tongues of Bondei, Digo, Nyakusa, Zigula and Shambala, through Zimbabwe in Lozi,

One of the first scientific illustrations of the baobab, this appeared in the volume of engravings accompanying the *Dictionnaire de botanique* by J B P A Lamarck, published in Paris in 1796. Lamarck was the first person to produce a reasoned theory of evolution.

Karanga, Zezuru and Shona. Like a trans-continental game of Chinese whispers, the word finally emerges at the southern end of the baobab's range in Limpopo province, in the Tshivenda language of South Africa, as *muvhuyu*.

Colloquial names have the licence to describe the very essence of a plant or animal with a lyricism not open to simple nouns, although 'baobab' does at least focus on the tree's many-seeded fruit. Most other names single out the white floury pith surrounding the seeds, which monkeys are not alone in enjoying. Several European names derive from the popularity of the pith, as either a refreshing drink – 'lemonade tree' – or a substitute for tartaric acid – 'cream-of-tartar tree' (*kremetartboom* in Afrikaans) or 'Ethiopian sour gourd'. However, none of these

THE AFRICAN BAOBAB

epithets has quite the poetry of the French *arbre de mille ans* (tree of a thousand years).

It would be at least 100 years after Adanson's description before British explorers began penetrating into eastern and southern Africa. They were unlikely to have been aware of the tree's existence as they embarked, unless they had read about it. First gracing bookshop windows in 1857, David Livingstone's *Missionary Travels* was one of the earliest accounts of African exploration and contained a two-page passage on the tree, which was clearly the same species Adanson had found in West Africa.

Whether most travellers recognized baobabs as such, or only identified them on their return home, their ingenuous astonishment on first seeing the

trees reverberates throughout one description after another, from Ibn Battuta, through Cadamosto to Michel Adanson and beyond. Typical was James Chapman in *Travels in the Interior of South Africa*. In 1852, accompanied by Thomas Baines, he found himself in northern Botswana, confronting one of his first baobabs:

'We were lost in amazement, truly, at the stupendous grandeur of this mighty monarch of the forest, in comparison with which the largest of hundreds of surrounding palm trees sunk into apparent insignificance.'

Thomas Baines painted this fine watercolour of a baobab in full leaf near Lake Ngami in northern Botswana in December 1861.

With African baobabs coming in such a variety of shapes and sizes, it is hardly surprising that there have been suggestions they comprise more than one species.

This tree was indeed a massive specimen, known as Chapman's baobab and protected under Botswana's Monuments and Relics Act. Its silhouette towered over the nearby fan palms (*Hyphaene petersiana*) and, until its collapse in 2016, this colossus lured many a weary or inquisitive traveller to its shade.

The bewildering variety in the shapes and sizes of both the trunks and fruit of baobabs gave several hopefuls enough reason to think they had found something fundamentally different from the tree described by Michel Adanson. The huge distance between the tropical coasts of East and West Africa, on both of which baobabs flourish, lent definite weight to the possibility of there being more than one species. Physical distance is often a precursor to genetic distance and, if populations have been separated long enough, their distinctive evolutionary trails will eventually begin to distinguish them.

In 1860 Britain's armchair explorers were reading *The Lake Regions of Central Africa* by Richard Burton. This polymath knew exactly what a baobab was when he wrote about it, and his extraordinary breadth of experience enabled him to make connections and comparisons nobody else possibly could. His name needed no immortalizing

THE AFRICAN BAOBAB

in a subspecies of *Adansonia digitata,* which makes his observations on the possibility of subspecific differences all the more valid:

> 'There appear to be two variations of this tree, similar in bole but differing in foliage and in general appearance. The normal Mbuyu has a long leaf, and the drooping outline of the mass is convex; the rarer, observed only upon the Usagara Mountains, has a small leaf, in colour like the wild indigo, and the arms striking upwardst assume the appearance of a bowl.'

But Burton was far ahead of his time and his enthusiasm for splitting species would be short-lived. A year before the publication of Burton's book, Charles Darwin had thrown the rock of *On the Origin of Species by Means of Natural Selection* into the pool of scientific philosophy. Species classification would never be the same again, as taxonomy was forced to look back to common ancestry, rather than at physical distinctions. So began a century of clumping hitherto separated races, subspecies, even species, together again. However, with DNA analysis and other microbiological studies becoming more accessible, the wheel may be turning full circle once more.

In December 2012, Jack D Pettigrew together with seven co-authors published a paper in the prestigious journal *Taxon,* entitled 'Morphology, ploidy and molecular phylogenetics reveal a new diploid species from Africa in the baobab genus *Adansonia'.* This species they named *Adansonia kilima',* the species name meaning 'hill' or 'mountain' in Swahili, referring to its altitudinal distribution in East and southern Africa at 650–1 500 m. As well

as investigating chromosome differences, the authors also noted distinctions in floral morphology, sufficient to convince themselves, at least, that they had identified a true new species.

Others, however, were not to be persuaded, and in the October 2016 volume of the same journal, Glynis V Cron and seven colleagues (including baobab guru, David Baum) published their rebuttal in 'One African baobab species or two? Synonymy of *Adansonia kilima* and *A. digitata'.* Here they concluded that 'there is no evidence of any [...] distinction between [the two types of baobab]' and this seems now to be the generally accepted position among most of the botanical community.

While scientists are counting chromosomes and comparing DNA, the Dogon and Bambara people in Mali are recognizing differences in bark colour, sufficient to give black-, grey- and red-barked baobabs different names. The distinctions in Mali extend beyond bark colour, as they do elsewhere in Africa, to fruit taste and suitability of bark fibre for ropes and baskets. In Botswana, a connection is made between pink-skinned trees and sweet pith, as it is in Tanzania by some of the Hadzabe.

As it so often seems to do, science is chasing after tradition.

This wind-blown tree on the Kenyan coastline is scarcely recognizable as a baobab.

CHAPTER TWO

A tree of Africa

Baobabs are quintessentially African
trees. It is possible they do not occur
naturally anywhere beyond the
continental mainland and some of its
outlying islands. However, the outline
of the species map is indistinct, and
we will never know for sure whether
some of the flourishing colonies along
its edges are due to the mobility of
mankind, or to the randomness of
natural seed dispersal.

It is hard to imagine a more African scene than this,
where the road leads off into the dusty distance,
and the baobab tree shows the scars of the attentions
of elephants.

THE AFRICAN BAOBAB

A TREE OF AFRICA

Native range of the trees

Roughly, indigenous baobabs grow naturally throughout continental Africa between the latitudes of 16° N and 26° S. The waterless wastes of the Sahara push down on the northern edges of their range and, although Khartoum in Sudan is almost within the baobab's native area, and seed pods may still be bought there in the market, the trees found there are introduced. To the south, the baobab's approximate limits are marked by the Limpopo basin in the east, and a line through northern Namibia in the west.

By overlaying the tree's optimum rainfall, temperature and altitude on this great belt of tropical Africa, as well as preferred drainage, soil types and other environmental influences, a very disjointed distribution map emerges. The most distinctive feature is the huge, unmarked space in the centre of the continent where no baobabs grow, and which effectively splits northern baobabs into two separate populations. Otherwise, baobabs are components of many different ecosystems, testifying to their tolerance of varying temperature, rainfall and soil type. Indeed, their habitats are so diverse that it is almost easier to define the trees' requirements by where they cannot live, rather than where they can.

There is no upper limit to the temperatures that baobabs tolerate, provided their soil and rainfall requirements are met. They grow easily in Mauritania and in the lowlands of Eritrea, where human inhabitants swelter in average summer temperatures of well over 30° C. At the other end of the thermometer, the baobab cannot endure the recurring spells of sustained frost that effectively demarcate much of its southern limits. However, this is not to say that baobabs, particularly mature specimens, cannot live through occasional freezing spells. Some of the biggest baobabs in Africa grow in northeastern Namibia, where temperatures regularly fall well below zero several nights in a row.

It takes more than just a general lack of frost to create a suitable environment for baobabs. They cover the northern slopes of the Soutpansberg

Approximate natural distribution of *Adansonia digitata*; it is impossible to know for certain whether or not the trees on the fringes of the species range are naturally distributed.

mountains of South Africa, spreading all the way down through mopane woodland to the Limpopo River. There being almost none on the southern slopes may be a consequence of differences in sunlight, temperature, rainfall, geology or some other more obscure needs of the tree that are unfulfilled on the shadier side of the mountains. Elsewhere on the continent, particularly in Kenya and Tanzania, the trees are absent from vast tracts of land where, superficially at least, conditions seem ideal.

Nowhere do baobabs live naturally much above 1 500 m. Yet the trees grow at this height as far north as northern Ethiopia. Around the equator, temperature ranges at higher altitudes are similar to those closer to sea level near the tropics. Why there is no sign of baobabs ever having colonized apparently suitable areas up to 2 000 m on the equator, where it is never anywhere near freezing, remains a wonderful mystery. Perhaps many months of cool nights are fatal to their fortunes, or long spells of grey damp days too much for tender young seedlings. Maybe there are fewer pollinators

THE AFRICAN BAOBAB

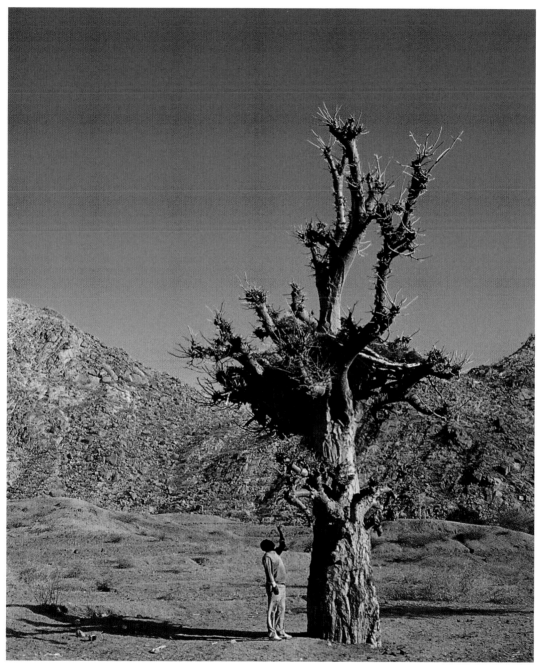

A baobab in the semi-desert of Eritrea growing at the extreme north of the species range; branches have been cut so leaves can be fed to livestock, while the tree itself is being used as a store for animal fodder.

Here, on the well-watered East African coast, the baobabs are part of a mosaic of much more varied vegetation than in drier parts of their range.

or seed dispersers at higher altitudes. If planted in well-drained soil, baobabs will just survive in Nairobi at nearly 2 000 m, and of the two specimens in the Nairobi Arboretum, one looks particularly healthy, with four strong trunks, each about the same circumference as the single trunk of the other tree. Both planted in 1922, neither has ever flowered, so something other than an absence of pollinators must be at work in stunting their development.

Temperature is merely one component of the environmental equation. Equally crucial is rainfall, and here the species shows true adaptability. Not only does the baobab survive in areas with very different rainfall averages, it also tolerates the successive years of extreme droughts and raging floods imposed by the unpredictability of African weather.

On the coast of Kenya, rainfall at Kilifi Plantations cattle and sisal farm averaged 1 170 mm over the last 50 years, More than half of the year's rain used to fall in the second quarter, the rest fairly evenly over the next six months, but now the vagaries of climate change have begun to upset the concept of average precipitation. Even when it isn't raining, humidity is high in Kilifi, but just 100 kilometres inland,

conditions are much harsher for baobabs growing around Tsavo National Park. There, drier areas receive less than a quarter of Kilifi's rainfall most years, often in two distinct seasons, and humidity is minimal. On parts of the west coast of the continent, the struggling baobabs in Mauritania must survive not only maximum temperatures and extreme water loss, but an average annual rainfall of less than 100 mm, in one short spell.

Baobabs growing outside their native range, like those in botanical gardens, often find themselves in areas of much higher rainfall than they would ever experience in their African homeland. These trees may spread out much quicker and larger, clearly demonstrating the connection between water consumption and growth, although too much rain may damn baobabs' survival chances just as effectively as too little. The maximum they can endure, year after year, seems to be about 1 400 mm (although the specimen in Calcutta's Botanical Garden tolerates a lot more). Baobabs are not forest trees, and young saplings are unable to compete with the luxuriant vegetation that grows in areas of heavy rainfall. This largely explains the

Because they grow in such shallow soil, these Kenyan coastal baobabs may be stunted, and therefore much older than they look.

THE AFRICAN BAOBAB

This west African baobab's roots are clearly washed by the sea, which seemingly has no adverse effects on the tree.

great blank in the heart of the African map, where the only baobabs occur around human habitations and, as such, are certainly imported.

Soil provides trees with nourishment and support, and its composition is fundamental to successful growth. There are few combinations of rock and soil that baobabs cannot eventually colonize, given suitable temperatures and rainfall, although soft, deep sand is not ideal, as it does not give roots sufficient support. A tree that appears to be growing successfully on the dunes is usually anchored to a layer of denser soil below the sand. With sands and coastlines shifting over time, it may have been much further from the sea when first sprouting from its seed. While tree roots are clearly better anchored in solid ground, surface soil can

sometimes seem almost superfluous. Baobabs often direct their roots down cracks in stony outcrops, gaining good support but very little nutrition. On the tiny islets between the cataracts of the Kunene River's spectacular Epupa Falls in northern Namibia, baobabs appear to live off water alone, their roots probing fissures in the rock in which there is little, if any, soil. Likewise, many trees along the East African coast are growing on no more than a few millimetres of decomposed vegetation, sprinkled over the rocky relics of much higher sea levels, their roots even washed by high water tides.

Given the tree's adaptability to such varied environments, it is impossible to extrapolate ideal natural conditions for baobab growth. Baobabs proclaim their success as a species in different

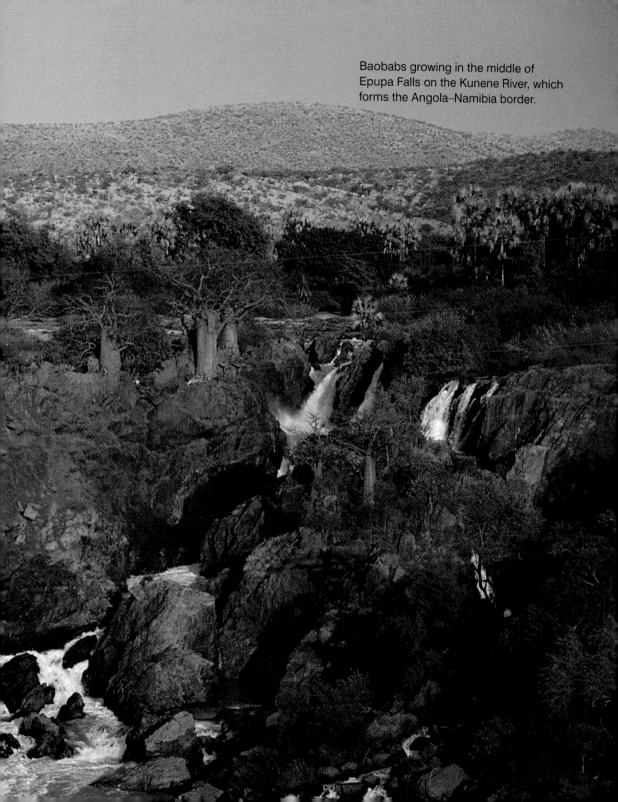

Baobabs growing in the middle of Epupa Falls on the Kunene River, which forms the Angola–Namibia border.

Baobab trees are easily assimilated into urban life, to the benefit of both tree and people.

ways. The localized monsters in Zimbabwe, Namibia or northern Botswana show that a thin layer of sand overlaying a non-porous base of calcrete is an ideal foundation for trees to reach enormous size. Yet the massed ranks of smaller baobabs in the valley of the Great Ruaha River are growing on steep, rocky slopes. And if a species' success were to be judged by a combination of numbers and size, parts of Senegal or the East African coastline seem to offer habitat that is little short of perfect.

Approaching natural baobab country, one is continually struck by the presence of outlying trees, far from the main aggregations – outriders fringing the edges of baobab populations, as if abandoned in the trees' retreat. These may be relicts of a much wider distribution, survivors from a different age, hanging on in the face of environmental degradation or warming climate, their ancestors long decayed. Two of Botswana's most famous baobab specimens, Green's and Chapman's, grew five kilometres from each other until the latter's collapse in 2016, but otherwise, there seemed to be no others within at least a day's walk of those trees.

It would be heartening to feel that some of these isolated trees actually evidence expansions of the baobab's natural range – early colonizers settling new territory rather than relicts staying on as their empire declines. Sadly, this doesn't seem to be so. A few seeds spat out by wandering travellers or crowds at a rural Zimbabwe bus stop may lead to trees growing where they never grew before. But ultimately, the influence of exploding populations of humans and their livestock on the baobab's fortunes cannot be other than destructive.

THE AFRICAN BAOBAB

The hand of humans

Historically, humankind's impact on baobabs has been more positive, and dense clumps where baobabs are otherwise sparsely spread often signify old human habitations. This connection between trees and humans is undeniable, although less clear is whether baobabs attracted people with shade and nourishment, or if the trees are there as a consequence of human activity.

As little as 5 000 years ago, giraffes were nibbling acacia branches throughout most of what is now desert. Almost certainly baobabs then grew far up into today's Sahara before a warming world slowly forced them into retreat. As the limits for both human and baobab survival were pushed southwards, humans may have depended on finding areas in which to live that were already populated with the trees.

Human activity is also likely to have encouraged more trees to grow. Once nomads adopted relatively settled lifestyles, they could have brought home pods from wild baobabs for food or medicine. Seeds are often sucked for the surrounding pith, or the two separated by vigorous stirring. Discarded seeds might have germinated around the villages, helped on their way with slops of dirty washing water.

Europeans frequently remarked upon the connection between baobabs and human habitations. The German Heinrich Barth is one of the unsung heroes of African exploration. He was introduced to Africa in 1849 as a member of a British anti-slavery expedition. His formal mission over, he began travelling on his own, making an astounding 19 000 km journey around Central Africa and the Sahel. His five-volume *Travels and Discoveries in North and Central Africa* makes particularly rich reading and is all the more remarkable for its publication in 1857, when Stanley was only 16, and Burton and Speke had yet to reach Lake Tanganyika. Barth's scientific leanings and powers of observation are evident in his comments:

Arrival of Dr. Barth at Timbuktu.

Barth may not have found baobabs in Timbuktu, but his observations on trees elsewhere were completely original.

'Here and there a large leafless Adansonia stretches forth its gigantic arms as if bewailing the desolation spread around, where human beings had formerly subsisted: for the Kuka or baobab likes the dwelling of the negro, and he, on the other hand, can scarcely live without it; for how could he season his simple food without the baobab's young fresh leaves, or sweeten and flavour his drink without the slightly acid pulp wherein the kernels are imbedded? It has been remarked by travellers that this tree is only found near some dwelling place of man; but I doubt whether we are authorised to regard all those specimens of it which are scattered over the wilds of central Africa as marking the site of former towns.'

Much later, in 1924, the writings of F W H Migeod appeared under the title *Through Nigeria to Lake Chad*. The author was also an acute observer, focusing as much on the people he encountered along his way as on the plants and animals. He was also a believer in the association between baobabs and human settlements, and he remarks on the baobab population in the area around Nigeria's Benue River that the tree . . .

'. . . has been imported by the Fulbe into these places and is not indigenous there. The mode of its dissemination is for the fruit to be carried on from the last tree to be eaten, for it is a favourite article of food, and the seeds thrown out germinate. Hence it is practically only in towns that it is found, and if found in the bush usually indicates the former presence of a village or camp.'

He then suggests, in describing his visit to Yola, eastern Nigeria, that knowing when humans first settled in a particular area could help age the surrounding baobabs '. . . as it is improbable that any [baobabs] were there before the Fulbe founded the town 100 years ago when they moved here from Gurin, the parent town'.

This is an interesting contrast to the ideas of the Giriama on the East African coast, who believe that only when a settlement is abandoned will baobabs begin to grow. They suggest that as long as domestic animals are nibbling at anything tender and green, or human and animal feet are flattening the surrounding ground, seedlings will never survive to grow into trees. C W Hobley, writing 'On Baobabs and Ruins' in the 1922 *Journal of the East Africa and Uganda Natural History Society*, reached the same conclusion, that only once 'the place was deserted owing to war or other causes, the bush would cover the area and the more recent baobab seeds would germinate along with other plants'.

Arabs founded their first African trading posts as early as 1 000 AD. Many of these were on islands such as Manda, Zanzibar and Kilwa. Others occupied mainland sites, often several kilometres from the sea. Some of these settlements were abandoned at least 500 years ago, the rest more recently. It is seldom clear whether the inhabitants were driven away by disease, warfare or water shortages. Mostly, only outlines of foundations remain – heat, rain and rampant vegetation having combined to reduce ancient townships to a few piles of overgrown stones. If it had not been for the towering presence of baobab trees betraying their existence, many of these sites might still lie undiscovered under tangles of creeping greenery.

Clumps of East African coastal baobabs may shade the burial sites of wandering Arab traders and imams. On the very edge of Mikindani Bay, near Tanzania's border with Mozambique, an Islamic holy man is buried in a one-man cemetery under a baobab. The oldest person I could find in the village remembered him praying daily beneath the tree. It seemed an appropriate resting place for the man's mortal remains. Here, tree clearly preceded grave, and perhaps also at the spectacular Tongoni Ruins burial ground much further north. There, on the slopes, below a tumbledown mosque, are the graves of at least 40 holy men. On the seaward side of the burial site are three beautiful baobabs, and the gravestones face down between their trunks to the sweep of mangrove-fringed coastline.

It is likely that old slave routes can be charted from strangely sited baobabs – just as borassus (*Borassus aethiopum*), doum (*Hyphaene compressa*) and other palms are supposed to reveal the ancient migration routes of elephants. Arab slave traders travelling from the coast are sure to

THE AFRICAN BAOBAB

Temple Point, on the Kenyan coast, clearly shows the connection between baobabs and Islamic worship.

have carried baobab fruit with them, as they did in their boats, spitting out pips along the way and so extending the baobab's range further inland, as well as marking their trails for posterity.

On the bigger island groups further off the coasts of Africa, the origins of healthy populations of baobabs are even less certain. Seed pods are said to have drifted on Indian Ocean currents to Aldabra, nearly 1 000 km from the mainland, and could have reached the Comoros, Mauritius and Réunion in the same way. On the other side of Africa, the Cape Verde Islands are so covered with baobabs it seems they must occur there naturally.

In addition to six endemic baobabs, groves of *Adansonia digitata* are also found in Madagascar. These trees nearly all grow along the island's west coast and are so clearly associated with human habitation that little doubt exists as to their introduction by humankind.

Of equally debatable origins are the few trees in Yemen and Oman. The presence of other African tree species in southwestern Arabia suggests baobabs could also have arrived there naturally, rather than in the dhows of Arab sailors.

In India, too, there are enough African baobabs to have caused much speculation on their origins.

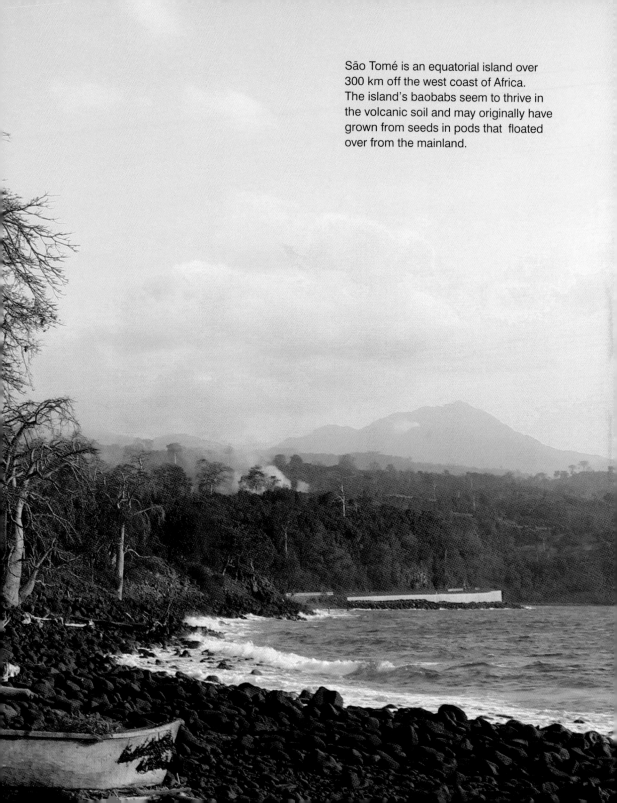

São Tomé is an equatorial island over 300 km off the west coast of Africa. The island's baobabs seem to thrive in the volcanic soil and may originally have grown from seeds in pods that floated over from the mainland.

If nature did not spread baobabs to India, there must be an explanation for their presence. It is easy to imagine seed pods bobbing over to Yemen, and even Oman is only a short float away compared to Australia, but if baobabs had drifted to India by sea, they would have established themselves there much earlier. They would also be most common down the west coast of the subcontinent, which they are not. It is more likely that they were imported by Arabs, which is the view of B H Baden-Powell, writing in the *Indian Forester* of 1878/9 that:

'The Tree was introduced into India from Tropical Africa (where it is indigenous) by Arab traders. Individual specimens have found their way as far north as Ajmir and the North-West Provinces. In Ajmir it is also called the "Kalp-briksh" or "Wishing Tree".'

This baobab in Mandu, Madhya Pradesh, India, probably owes its presence to Arab traders.

One of the most telling arguments in favour of a comparatively recent arrival is the lack of a Sanskrit name for the tree, or indeed any name that is not merely a hybrid of two older words with other meanings. *Khurasani imli* is one of the Hindi names for baobab in Uttar Pradesh, which, loosely translated, means the 'foreign tamarind'. Other names incorporate salmali, the Sanskrit name for the kapok-like, red silk-cotton tree (*Ceiba* spp.). There is no mention of the baobab in ancient Indian botanical texts, nor are there long-established uses for any part of the tree. If it really was part of India's botanical heritage, such lack of written record or traditional usage is inconceivable.

This was the generally accepted wisdom of the time, and it is still possible to correlate areas where baobabs are commonest with those parts of India most under the influence of Islam. For thousands of years Arabs traded their way around the Indian Ocean rim, and almost certainly carried baobab fruit with them, probably as an on-board source of vitamin C. In addition to discarding any surplus when they docked, they may also have sought to spread their sources of supply by encouraging Indians to plant the trees for shade, medicine, decoration, or food.

The slave trade was the catalyst for the spread of baobabs all over the Caribbean and South America, vitamin-rich seed pods coming over on boats during the forced African diaspora. Well over 100 baobabs have been catalogued in and around Recife in northeast Brazil, almost certainly originally imported by Dutch slavers. Until recently, there

THE AFRICAN BAOBAB

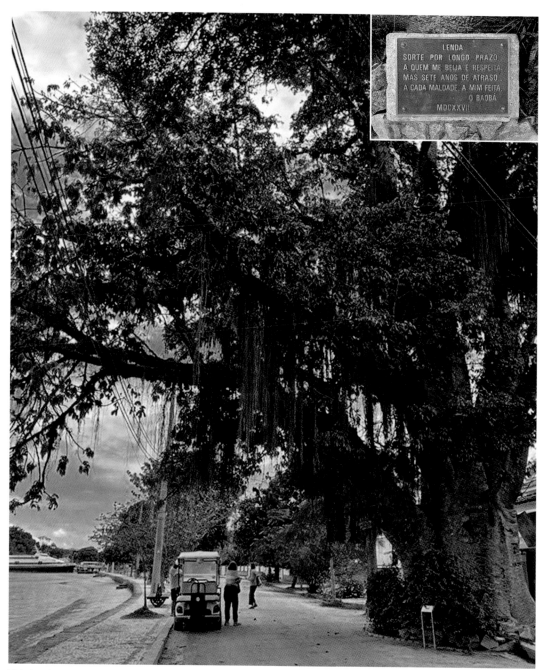

LENDA
SORTE POR LONGO PRAZO,
A QUEM ME BEIJA E RESPEITA,
MAS SETE ANOS DE ATRASO,
A CADA MALDADE, A MIM FEITA.
O BAOBÁ
MDCXXVII

This baobab is growing on the Island of Paquetá in Guanabara Bay, Rio de Janeiro. Its plaque's translation reads: 'Long-term luck to those who kiss and respect me. But a seven-year curse for every harm done to me'.

A TREE OF AFRICA

43

This baobab in Queen's Park, Bridgetown, Barbados is unlikely to be 1 000 years old, as claimed, but rather grew from a seed brought over on one of the early slave boats.

were only two baobabs in Barbados. One of them, claimed to be the oldest, stands near Warrens, once a great plantation house but now engulfed by the expansion of Bridgetown. *Flora Barbadia* quotes an early European history of the Island suggesting the tree dates to around 1735 and sprouted from a seed brought over from Guinea. Much larger is the specimen in Queen's Park, with a trunk so impressive it is difficult to believe it doesn't predate the arrival of the first slaves around 1630.

Baobabs are also mentioned in an early version of *Flora of Dutch West Indian Islands* as occurring in St Eustatius and St Martin, and they are found in Trinidad too. Guinea also seems to have been the source of trees in Tobago, judging from the baobab's colloquial name there of 'Guinea tamarind'.

The further away from Africa baobabs grow, the more assured is their exotic status. They thrive in Guyana, on the north coast of South America, and many are now found in southern Florida, the seeds apparently imported from Cuba, and that island's from Haiti. In turn, Haitian baobabs derive from seeds brought over from Africa on slave boats or by immigrants of French descent.

Baobabs need more than just a human helping hand to disperse them if they are to survive very far beyond the tropics. The baobab in the Kirstenbosch Botanical Gardens outside Cape Town owes its size to the warmth of a glasshouse. The species' exotic status in England has never been in question; its introduction there goes back 300 years, to 1724, when George I was on the throne.

THE AFRICAN BAOBAB

Philip Miller (1691–1771) tended the Botanick Garden in Chelsea for the Worshipful Company of Apothecaries. His *Gardener's Dictionary* went into eight editions, and in the seventh edition (1764) he describes the first importation of baobabs into England:

'The plants have been many years in England, yet none of them have produced Flowers, so that we are at a loss for the Characters. We have some plants of this sort in several gardens which were raised from Seeds obtained from Grand Cairo in the Year 1724, by the late Dr William Sherrard, many of which were grown to the Height of eighteen Feet; but in the severe Winter of 1740, they were all lost, and since that Time there has not been any of the Seeds brought to England, till the return of Mr Adanson to Paris, who sent some of the Seeds over here, which have succeeded and many of the Plants are now upwards of six Feet high.'

In tropical botanical gardens all around the world, baobabs display bloated trunks and wrinkled skins to unbelieving visitors. Sometimes local fruit bats or hawkmoths will visit the flowers and ensure that seed pods eventually bedeck the branches of these exotic imports. While such representatives of their species can hardly be said to be extending its range, they certainly create greater public awareness of the existence of this botanical marvel.

THE

GARDENER'S AND BOTANIST'S DICTIONARY;

CONTAINING

THE BEST AND NEWEST METHODS OF CULTIVATING AND IMPROVING THE

KITCHEN, FRUIT, AND FLOWER GARDEN, AND NURSERY;

OF PERFORMING THE

PRACTICAL PARTS OF AGRICULTURE;

OF MANAGING VINEYARDS,

AND

OF PROPAGATING ALL SORTS OF TIMBER TREES.

BY THE LATE

PHILIP MILLER, F.R.S.

GARDENER TO THE WORSHIPFUL COMPANY OF APOTHECARIES AT THEIR BOTANIC GARDEN IN CHELSEA, AND MEMBER OF THE BOTANIC ACADEMY AT FLORENCE.

TO WHICH ARE NOW FIRST ADDED,

A COMPLETE

ENUMERATION AND DESCRIPTION OF ALL PLANTS HITHERTO KNOWN,

WITH THEIR

GENERIC AND SPECIFIC CHARACTERS,

PLACES OF GROWTH, TIMES OF FLOWERING, AND USES BOTH MEDICINAL AND ECONOMICAL.

THE WHOLE CORRECTED AND NEWLY ARRANGED,

WITH THE ADDITION OF ALL THE MODERN IMPROVEMENTS IN LANDSCAPE GARDENING, AND IN THE CULTURE OF TREES, PLANTS, AND FRUITS,

PARTICULARLY IN THE VARIOUS KINDS OF HOT HOUSES AND FORCING FRAMES;

WITH PLATES EXPLANATORY BOTH OF THEM, AND THE PRINCIPLES OF BOTANY.

BY

THOMAS MARTYN, B.D. F.R.S.

REGIUS PROFESSOR OF BOTANY IN THE UNIVERSITY OF CAMBRIDGE.

IN TWO VOLUMES.

VOL. I. PART I. A—CIV.

LONDON:

PRINTED FOR F. C. AND J. RIVINGTON, J. JOHNSON, G. AND W. NICOL, R. BALDWIN, W. J. AND J. RICHARDSON, J. HAYES, R. FAULDER AND SON, T. PAYNE, W. LOWNDES, J. WALKER, G. WILKIE AND J. ROBINSON, CUTHELL AND MARTIN, R. LEA, VERNOR, HOOD, AND SHARPE, J. TAYLOR, R. JEFFERY, W. CLARKE AND SONS, G. ROBINSON, C. LAW, J. WHITE, LONGMAN, HURST, REES AND ORME, CADELL AND DAVIES, J. MURRAY, W. STEWART, J. BOOTH, S. BAGSTER, AND I. BOOKER;

BY LAW AND GILBERT, ST. JOHN'S SQUARE, CLERKENWELL

M DCCC VII.

Philip Miller's *Gardener's Dictionary* was the first publication to write about the importation of baobabs into England.

Even in Africa, the demarcation of baobab territory owes much to human rather than natural history. Further away, particularly in India and the West Indies, the tree flourishes thanks to the early popularity of its fruit, and by most standards is a net gain to its new environment. Whether baobabs are indigenous or exotic, the relationship between humans and tree seems, at least for most of their joint existence, to have worked for the benefit of both.

These are large baobabs, even though
they are growing in almost no soil, and like
many others along the African coast, they
seem to flourish despite the salty spray.

Flower and seed

Like animals, plants begin life at the critical moment of conception. Whether baobab, butterfly or baboon, new life only starts when a male cell joins a female, when sperm makes contact with an egg. For butterflies or baboons, copulation is the prelude to conception. For flowering plants, it is pollination – when that great extravagance, the flower, tempts birds, insects and other animals with colour and scent into unconsciously shifting dust from the stamen of one bloom to the stigma of another.

This perfect flower shows its stigma on the end of the style, protruding through the mass of pollen-tipped stamens.

Flowers

Young baobab trees need all their energy for growing and have none to spare for reproduction. In their natural state, baobabs may be near 30 years old before they begin diverting vitality into producing flowers, and their first waxy white blooms appear. These blooms are striking, in both size and design, their magnificence in shining contrast to the stark grey tree that produces them, particularly when flowers appear on bare branches. Programmed by the tree's hormones to stay open for no longer than a single night and into the next morning, these are surely one of nature's more elaborate excesses.

Before a flower breaks open, the petals (corolla) and the other parts deeper inside are squeezed tightly into a spherical bud about the size of a golf ball. The outside of the bud (calyx) is made up of protective, dark greenish-yellow sepals with a velvety texture. When the flower is about to open, the calyx splits into sepals, which curve outwards to reveal five (occasionally four or six) crinkly white petals. The sepals unfold in a smooth, slow motion, and the flower takes less than half an hour to reach its full flamboyance.

Within the petals is an orb of hundreds of stamens, each tipped with an anther that produces pollen. Through the cluster of stamens protrudes the much longer style, ending in the stigma, the receptive end of the female reproductive organ. Pollination is the process of transferring male pollen from stamens to stigma. At the other end of the stigma is the ovary, inside which the egg cells rest. Once deposited on the stigma, pollen shoots down a long tube through the style, the sperm then travelling quickly down to fertilize the eggs. Successful conception soon becomes evident in the appearance of a tiny pod encasing a capsule of small white seeds.

Baobabs are bisexual, or perfect, in botanical terms, in that there are male stamens and a female style on each flower, unlike unisexual or imperfect

A cross section of a baobab flower clearly showing the style down which fertilization takes place.

flowers that have either one or the other. Perfect plants are more prone to self-pollination, although some have evolved devices to encourage cross- rather than self-pollination, and so boost the creation of the new genetic combinations that are the raw material for natural selection.

Dena Elijah is a guide at the Gedi Ruins on Kenya's coast, and for a long time had noticed that in his nearby village of Jimba, of the two baobabs growing there, one regularly bore almost no fruit, despite flowering profusely, while its neighbour fruited well, particularly on the side next to the first tree. Others living around baobabs have long made similar observations, and now science is beginning to offer some explanations. In Volume 489, June 2021, of the journal *Forest Ecology and Management*, A. Chetty and four others published a paper entitled 'Reproductive ecology of the African baobab: Floral features differ among individuals with different fruit production'. Their study concluded

It will not be long before these flowers fall; their brown marks suggest they were visited by pollinators during the night.

that baobabs that fruited well had better-developed female styles and stigmas, while those that produced little or no fruit had flowers with more numerous and prominent male stamens.

Flowering is the curtain-raiser to the main act of seed production, and its timing is critical. Near the tropics, where seasons are distinct, lengthening days or warmer temperatures may provide the necessary stimuli, and the appearance of leaves in October or November, and flowers shortly thereafter, is predictable. On the equator, seasonal temperatures vary less, and day lengths are constant enough for the Swahili clock to measure time by 12 hours of day and 12 of night all year round. There, more obscure environmental signals trigger the appearance of the great white blooms, which usually begin to show before the onset of the rains. Flowers often appear before the leaves have started budding, when not only the baobabs, but almost every other tree around them, are bare-branched, and the entire grey-brown landscape anticipates the rain.

Occasional flowers may show at almost any time in the tree's annual cycle. In Mali, at the end of April, the lightning storms along the Bandiagara Escarpment in Dogon country can be spectacular – forks, sheets and flashes in an almost continuous two-hour show of *lumière* without the sun. The storms are dry too, and the wind that follows brings only sand, not moisture. The year I visited, every baobab tree was still nearly moribund, and absolutely bare, almost as if reluctant to risk flowering in that parched countryside until rain actually started falling.

The highlight of the day's walk to Tireli was the crocodile pool, where saurian relics of the last Ice Age were still said to linger, hundreds of desiccated semi-desert miles from their nearest fellows. That they sometimes did was clear from the little dead one at the mouth of a hole, but the pool was dusty dry, and we were told its inhabitants had retreated into spring-fed shelters high up the cliffs. Near the pool stood a group of baobabs, all as bare as each

Neither leaf, flower nor fruit adorn this tree and the most these buffalo can hope for is some dappled midday shade.

other – except for one. On a low branch, within stretching distance, was a single glorious flower.

The one-night chance for that Malian flower to lure a nocturnal pollinator was over, and its unblemished petals suggested it had failed in nature's purpose. Soon its redundant corolla of discarded petals would slide down the style and drop to the ground, like millions of others are doing somewhere, most African mornings. Almost as if scorched by the sun's rays, all these fallen flowers will soon start to crumple, turning first a dirty brown, then a deep russet red.

Flowering before the rains start is risky. The advantage of doing so lies in being able to tempt pollinators with food in dry weather when there is little else for them to choose from. However, if the rains fail there may not be enough water to sustain seed growth, although this is less hazardous for baobabs, which store large amounts of water in their trunks, than it is for other native species.

Baobabs in Kenya are divided into two distinct populations. At the coast most flower just before the long rains in April or May, bursting into leaf soon thereafter. Inland, some hormonal signal stimulates baobabs into blooming by the time the short rains start in October. Maverick trees in either population often keep time to their own biological clocks, flowering long before all the other baobabs around them, or coming into leaf when none of the others are.

Baobab flowers are open for about 18 hours, and for most of that time it is dark. Belying their beauty, they have an acrid smell that hints at something rotten, although there seems to be no English word that readily describes the smell, nor any odour with which it can easily be compared. Writers clutch at sensory straws in describing it as 'cabbagey' or 'like sour watermelon, urine, mice or sweaty feet'. None of the several authors of popular botanical books describing baobab flowers as

This picture of buds, flower and pods all together shows how it is often impossible to attribute distinct flowering and fruiting seasons to any population of baobabs.

THE AFRICAN BAOBAB

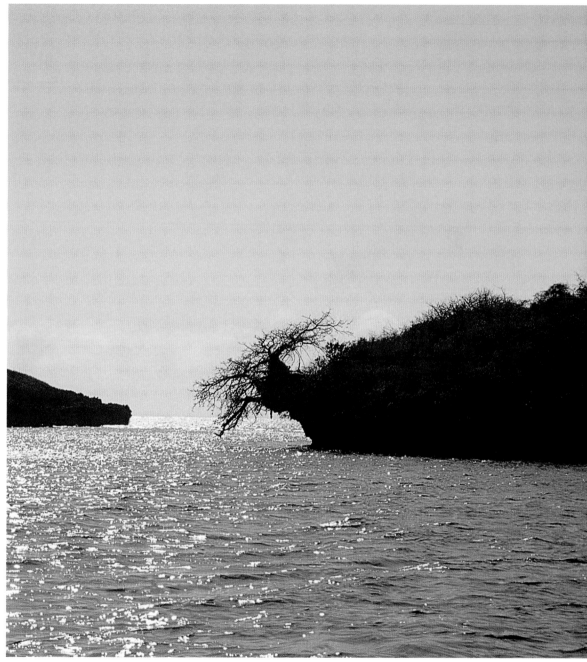

Hanging over the waters of the Indian Ocean on a tiny coral outcrop near the Kenya–Somali border, this tree must surely have emerged from a seed that was dispersed by the sea.

'sweetly scented' can ever have smelt them. Perhaps they have been beguiled by the magnificence of the photographed flower into believing it cannot be other than exquisitely perfumed.

Doyens of South African dendrology, Fried and Jutta von Breitenbach, camped under a baobab tree near the Zimbabwe border for four weeks in November 1972. They published their observations in the April–June 1974 issue of *Trees in South Africa*. The tree was already in full leaf, and began flowering the day they arrived, continuing to do so until just before they left.

Each evening the first buds started to crack at around 18:30 and within 20 minutes the sepals had curled back to reveal the mass of petals. These then unfolded to release the ball of stamens through which protruded the style. During the night the petals lifted still higher, like wings, further exposing the stamens to the attentions of nocturnal visitors. The next morning the process went into reverse, the closing sepals pressing the darkening petals back around the stamens, the whole tired and wilted flower then sliding down the style to the ground.

Most of the flowers on this tree will have fallen off by the time new ones start opening in the evening.

Like the flowers of baobab trees, those of the sausage tree *Kigelia africana* are pollinated by bats, and these huge fruits, which can weigh up to seven kilos, are the end result.

Pollination

Flowers evolve to balance the energy cost of blooming for a given length of time against the likelihood of receiving a visit from a pollinator while they are receptive. Pollination is a hit and miss affair at the best of times, one of nature's particularly chancy strategies. Where pollinators are scarce, or only visit flowers sporadically each day, as in temperate climates, flowers help their reproductive prospects by staying open much longer than they do near the equator. There, prolific animal, bird and insect life mean baobab flowers can open for just a few hours and still have a good chance of attracting pollinators.

Bats are either frugivorous or insectivorous, and it took a long time before botanists could say, with some scientific certainty, that they were the African baobab's prime pollinator. Bat pollination (chiropterophily) is unusual, and trees so pollinated show a number of distinctive design features. The flowers need to open at night and must appeal more to a bat's olfactory senses than to its less-efficient sense of sight. This sense of smell responds to odours that seem unappealing to humans, like the acrid scent of a baobab flower, which may have evolved to resemble that of a bat. Bat-pollinated flowers should also be robust enough to allow the mammals to cling onto petals or stamens while eating pollen or lapping up nectar – of which these flowers usually produce large amounts. Crucially, the flowers must also be easy for bats to reach, growing on the ends of branches or long stalks so the visitors can easily swoop down in the dark without becoming entangled in twigs and leaves. The flowers of all other species of baobab grow on much shorter stalks, protruding either erectly or horizontally off the branches. Such orientation is ill-suited to bat visits and the blooms rely on birds and insects to spread their pollen.

Sausage trees (*Kigelia africana*) often grow in the same parts of Africa as baobabs. Not only do these trees share the obvious characteristic of producing big, heavy fruit, but both are also bat pollinated. The sausage tree's exquisite crimson flowers have a smell that is also very unappealing to humans. They hang down off stalks that are anything from two to seven metres long, around which bats can easily flutter. The kapok or silk-cotton tree (*Ceiba pentandra*) is closely related to the baobab and bat-pollinated as well, and having been introduced from South America into Africa and elsewhere further east has no trouble attracting the local fruit-bats to pollinate its pale flowers.

Chiropterophily is a tropical phenomenon generally, and in Africa many of the bats that sip baobab or sausage tree nectar do so largely because there is no fruit around when these trees

The Egyptian fruit bat is one of the prime pollinators of baobab flowers.

are flowering. Two particular species of fruit bat are identified as frequent baobab pollinators. One is the straw-coloured fruit bat (*Eidolon helvum*), which often roosts colonially in town parks. The other is the Egyptian fruit bat (*Rousettus aegyptiacus*), which has evolved a simple echolocation system, unusual for fruit bats, but typical for the cave-rooster that it is. As lots of bats roosting together quickly exhaust nearby food supplies, they need to forage far from their home cave or grove of trees. Baobabs growing a long way from roosts, therefore, still have good chances of attracting passing bats with their pungent flowers.

On the south coast of Kenya is the small fishing village of Msambweni, which lends its name to four kilometres of nearby beach. At one end of the beach the sand gives way to a rocky headland of fossilized coral reef, beyond which is a jumble of cracks, caves and chimneys that make an ideal roost for bats. Thousands of mostly Egyptian fruit bats emerge in the early evening before heading up or down the coast to feed.

At the other end of Msambweni beach, close to the village, is a beautiful grove of baobabs on the edge of a football pitch. When I visited there one December at twilight, a single baobab was already in full flower with buds on other trees just opening. Within minutes of my arrival, 20 or 30 bats appeared. It was bewitching to watch them scrabbling and twittering around the tree, backed by the rising moon's reflection in the silvery-black sea. They would swoop down onto the outlying branches – the flowers were unrecognizable as such in the dark – cling on with flapping wings for just a few seconds, then fall away and flit off to find more nectar.

Individual baobab trees are usually sparing with their blooms each night, and few flowers open at once. This prompts bats to move from tree to tree – so promoting cross-pollination – rather than to feast on a single tree and merely move pollen from one of its flowers to another. By the staggered flowering of trees in the same population, and at least a few flowers on any single tree opening every night for up to six weeks, the supply of baobab nectar is effectively prolonged, and pollinators are kept interested enough to return. The tree observed by the Von Breitenbachs produced about 400 flowers over the course of four weeks.

Bats leave clear evidence of nocturnal visits to baobab flowers in their claw marks, which are

While baobab flowers last little longer than 24 hours on the tree, once they dry out on the ground they can remain intact for weeks.

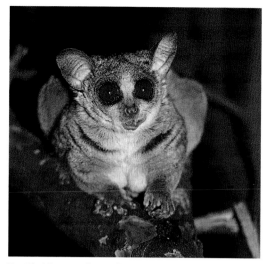

Bushbabies or galagos (here, a lesser galago) are occasional pollinators of baobab flowers.

already dark-edged the next morning. Baobab petals are particularly rich in tannin. This oxidizes very quickly, turning the whole petal brown in a few hours. The fallen petals are resilient and remain easily recognizable as recent components of baobab flowers, even after being rained upon. Slowly, they dry out into brittle chestnut crisps that litter the earth around the trees for many weeks after falling.

Bushbabies (galagos) have also been observed pollinating baobabs while munching petals or sipping nectar. They may be locally effective pollinators, but in the greater scheme of things they are too few, and too sparsely distributed, to do more than act as occasional agents of pollen transfer. Like most mammals that don't fly, they make poor cross-pollinators, and if they move pollen from the stamens of one flower to the stigma of another it is most likely to be between flowers on the same tree.

Hawkmoths have been found to play a much greater role in fertilizing baobab flowers than was supposed, particularly in southern Africa, where they are much more important pollen-shifters than bats. Giant carpenter bees crawl all over the orb of stamens; honeybees clamber more delicately along

the surface of the flower, collecting pollen; ants rush around the petals and even bluebottles seem to be attracted by the rotting smell of fading flowers. These insects may be gathering pollen or may inadvertently collect it on their bodies. However, they usually move on without leaving any on the flower's style, which protrudes so far beyond the stamens that most insects seldom come into contact with its tip.

Hawkmoths are the principal pollinators of the intricate flowers of Madagascar's *Adansonia za*.

The majority of seeds from
most fruits will never germinate.

Seed pods

Young seed pods look like large green or browny-green plums, then apples, before taking on more familiar cucumber, marrow or melon shapes. Starting off pale green, they slowly darken and harden, becoming more grey or yellow. Stalk lengths differ, too, seeming to vary with the size of the fruit they support.

There are still some spectacular baobabs in northeastern Namibia, although the Grootboom ('big tree' in Afrikaans) that grew near Tsumkwe has now collapsed. In its day, this was surrounded by several smaller trees and when I visited in August, one of these attendants had distinctly pink bark, quite different in colour from the other grey-trunked trees. To add strength to the contention that differently coloured baobabs may be genetically distinct, the fruits of the pink Namibian tree were exceptionally elongated, in obvious contrast to the less cylindrical baubles dangling off other nearby baobabs. Further observations have convinced me that individual trees always produce the same-shaped fruit, year after year.

Among hundreds of trees around Kilifi on the Kenyan coast, after a long rainy season was easing off into scattered July squalls, most pods were like huge fat marrows, but there were some distinct oddities among them. Some trees had grown fruit

The magnificent illustrations in *Flore d'Amerique*, published around 1843, were from the hand of Etienne Dennise, who, having lived in the West Indies, was well aware that baobabs were not indigenous there.

Baobab pods come in all shapes and sizes, but their inside design of pith, seeds and fibres remains the same.

THE AFRICAN BAOBAB

contoured somewhere between a giant comma and a human foetus – quite like expanded versions of the kidney-shaped seeds within them. Another tree was losing its greenery long before most of the others, giving it a sickly look by comparison with its lustrous neighbours. Among its remaining leaves hung seed pods shaped like tubular balloons, each with a small, unfilled nipple at the end, tipped with the remnants of the wizened style.

Internally, pods are divided lengthways into sections by the coarse brown fibres that have channelled nourishment to growing seeds. Within each section, seeds nestle comfortably into the vitamin C-rich pith that supports them. Seeds are not easily parted from their pith, but once they are, appear as dark brown kidney beans, about a centimetre long, with soft, nutty-tasting centres.

Botanically speaking, pods are described as 'indehiscent', meaning they do not open spontaneously while still on the tree. (One of the characteristics of the Australian boab, distinguishing it from all other species in the genus, is that pods crack open before they fall.) The fruit of *Adansonia digitata* may hang on the tree for a very long time, yet no matter how reluctant the tree is to let them go, they never open on the branches.

Fallen pods usually remain intact when they drop, slowly drying out as their shells become increasingly brittle. Then rot sets in and, by the time the next crop of pods is ripe, all that remains of the previous year's fruit are scattered fragments of the outer casing.

Large pods may weigh over 2 kg and contain more than 400 seeds – the most I have counted in Kenya was 462. These are super-fruit compared to those in drier parts of Africa, where seed numbers in tiny, apple-sized pods may not even reach double figures. If the pods lie where they land, the rotting shells are soon invaded by ants, termites and brightly coloured cotton-stainer bugs, all bringing in soil and moisture. Crush a fallen pod, and it is often already full of the damp earth that provides such an ideal environment for seed germination.

Top: The petals and stamens have slipped down the style to the ground. If pollination has been successful the ovary will soon start to enlarge. **Above:** These petals and stamens have caught on the end of the style and will remain there as the fruit continues to ripen.

Seed dispersal

Any seed pod's contents are far more useful to the species when spread away from the plant that produced them. Many big trees have vast splaying webs of roots, so that even if seeds germinated where they fell, they could scarcely survive to compete with their parent. Nature provides external agents to disperse seeds, either in the random form of wind, water or passing creatures, or in the deliberate actions of animals eating seeds, which they expel elsewhere. Seeds are often coated with fruit, which acts as an inducement to birds or animals to swallow them, the journey through digestive systems ultimately helping them germinate.

Baboons either feast up in the tree, pulling fruit from the branches, or carry pods off and crack them open in solitary peace some distance away.

This baobab had two particular attractions for baboons: it was the only tree in fruit for kilometres around, and the baboons were able to reach its branches by first climbing the adjacent thorn tree.

THE AFRICAN BAOBAB

The bright chestnut fibres are a clear sign of fresh fruit having been recently opened by baboons.

Monkeys love the pith in baobab pods – the vitamin-rich coating on the indigestible pill. It takes the jaws of a baboon to break open a big baobab fruit, and smaller monkeys may have to make do with fallen, weaker-shelled pods. Baboons invade fruiting baobabs with the enthusiasm of locusts for a field of greenery. One April I found nearly 50 baboons adorning almost the only tree in Tanzania's Tarangire National Park, which was leafless and in fruit. They are noisy creatures and seem compelled to accompany every activity with snarls and screams, sounding far more vicious than they really are. Yet this pith must be the manna that sustains them in their wilderness, and with concentration that left no room for bickering, they would pull a pod off a branch and crack it open in their jaws. Then they picked away at the contents with their hands, just like their human relations dipping into packets of crisps. The only sound from the tree was the drip, drip, of discarded bits of shell, hitting the ground with the staccato rhythm of raindrops falling off the leaves after a passing storm.

Baobab trunks are often too smooth for baboons to climb, but these monkeys started gingerly down the trunk, tail first, and then leapt onto a nearby acacia tree, which they descended with ease. Once on terra firma they behaved in more conventional baboon fashion, scrapping over fallen fruit and aggressively preserving their pecking order. Often one would scamper off onto the rocky slopes nearby, seed pod in jaws, there to eat quietly on its own, away from the frenzy of communal baboon existence. Baboons are after the pith, and sometimes frustrate nature's design by spitting out the seeds. Usually, though, they eat the entire contents of the pod, and in this way, seeds reach the stony areas where the baboons like to rest, and where young seedlings have a better chance of not being eaten by livestock or trampled by game animals.

Swallowed seeds are easily identifiable in baboon droppings. Walking up the edge of the Athi River in Tsavo National Park, I came to a patch of sand where a party of baboons had obviously rested, lots of bean-shaped baobab seeds showing clearly in their droppings. All the trees I had seen so far were without either pods or leaves, but this meant a nearby one must be in fruit, and, as if to confirm this, close to another pile of droppings were scattered pieces of pod shell. I could not

Baobab seeds are still easily recognizable after passing through the digestive system of a baboon, and are more likely to germinate having done so.

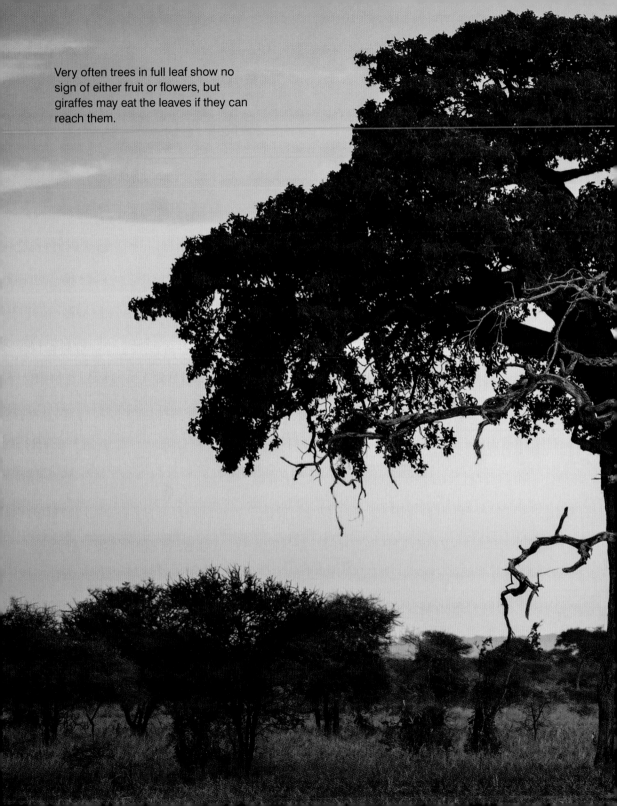

Very often trees in full leaf show no sign of either fruit or flowers, but giraffes may eat the leaves if they can reach them.

see the fruiting tree until I was well away from the river, and not before first finding more bits of shell, the attached fibres still bright chestnut. The pods had recently been opened and canine teeth marks showed clearly. The baboons had been eating fallen fruit, rather than climbing the tree to feast. Fruit ripped straight off branches comes away with twigs and strips of bark, whereas withered stalks were still attached to these pods, showing them to have ripened and fallen naturally.

Where baboons are scarce, baobab seeds will not get the transport to distant cliffs or rocky kopjes so crucial to the species' future. Today's arable farmers cannot afford baboons rampaging through their crops, and the primate's dwindling numbers must inevitably bring about a shrinkage in the range of the tree. One of many possible reasons for the very restricted distribution of Madagascar's baobabs may be their having evolved to rely for dispersal of their seeds on the appetites of elephant birds, giant tortoises or giant lemurs, all of which are now extinct. A recent analysis of the fallen fruits of *Adansonia rubistropa* found very little evidence of any animals presently dispersing seeds, other than rats' teeth marks on the shells, and concluded that 'the Malagasy baobab species are vulnerable to the loss of primary seed dispersers'.

African elephants may eat whole pods, or their contents, although reports of their doing so are scarce, and the pachyderms mainly focus their often-destructive energies on the trees' trunks. Mice, rats, squirrels and other small mammals certainly contribute to the dispersal of baobab seeds, at least beyond the tree canopy where they fall. Water also carries baobab pods down rivers and around lake shores, but not to the same extent it disperses the seeds of doum palms or coconuts. Baobabs growing on islands in the middle of wide African rivers are unquestionably spread by water.

Elephants seldom seem to eat baobab pods, preferring to strip the tree trunk for its moisture.

THE AFRICAN BAOBAB

FLOWER AND SEED

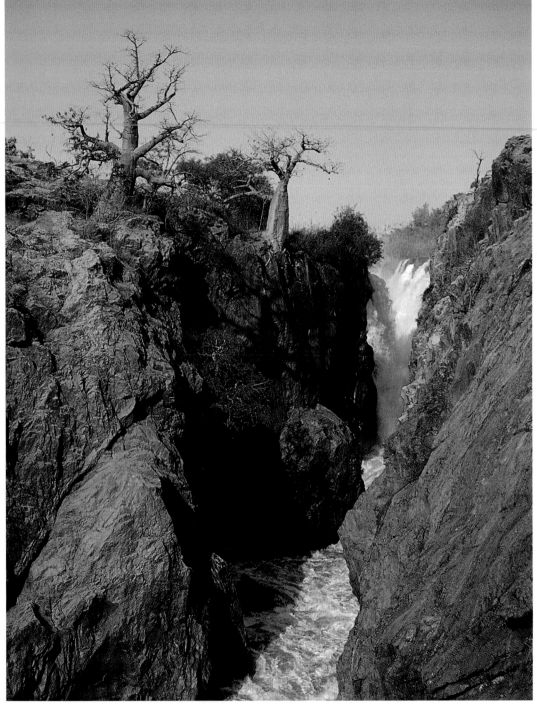

The seeds from which these trees grow on the banks of the Kunene River were probably deposited when the river was in full flood.

THE AFRICAN BAOBAB

The Kunene River originates in the highlands of Angola, and its lower reaches form the boundary with Namibia. The Epupa Falls are the visual high point of this river's journey to the sea. Between the tumble of different cataracts are tiny rocky islets, to many of which small baobabs cling – surely among the best-watered specimens on the continent.

Baobabs live to great ages. In their early years their fruits will be small and few, increasing in size and number as the trunk thickens and branches lengthen. Perhaps an average baobab first fruits aged 30, and then once a year for the next 200 years. And perhaps it produces between 20 and 500 pods every time it bears fruit, with an average of 300 every year over those 200 years. Each of these pods contains a dry-country average of 100 seeds – an average total of 30 000 seeds each year for 200 years, making a lifetime's output of six million. A single common oak tree (*Quercus robur*) has been estimated to produce five million acorns in what may be a similar lifespan.

To keep any population of mature baobabs or oaks at its present level, each individual specimen needs to produce one offspring that survives to fruit by the time its parent dies. So, one mature tree needs to grow from the six million seeds produced by an average baobab during an average lifespan. Numbers of seeds might naturally seem to affect numbers of trees, but this vast surplus makes the connection extremely tenuous. Most seeds never germinate, either failing to attract the attentions of a dispersal agent or falling on the proverbial stony ground, even if they do. Others will germinate and start to shoot, synthesizing water and carbon dioxide into nourishment for herbivorous mammals.

While producing baobab seeds by the million may seem wasteful from a baobab perspective, either they, or the emerging seedlings, serve to nourish the multitudes of other creatures living in baobab country, otherwise they rot away, fertilizing the ground around the tree that produced them. Indeed, it is just as well that baobabs, or any other naturally occurring species, are not too successful. If, during their lives, each breeding baobab produced even five saplings that survived to maturity, after two generations there would be 25 times as many baobabs smothering the savanna. This may be fine for baobabs but the population explosion could only be bought at the price of driving out many other plants from the savanna mosaic – and bringing us one step closer to turning into reality the alarming scenario in Antoine de Saint-Exupery's *Le Petit Prince* – that 'if the planet is too small, and if the baobabs are too numerous, they will finally make the planet explode'.

Le Petit Prince is one of the most popular books in the world. The prince would like to find a sheep to eat all the baby baobabs before they overrun his planet!

CHAPTER FOUR

Life and death

It is tough for a tree trying to gain a roothold on the open plains of the savanna or the flatlands of fossilized coral reef along the coastline. Scarcely any part of Africa is left ungrazed by wild game or herds of domestic livestock. Being protected by neither thorns nor a foul taste, baobab shoots are prime food. Human populations outside national parks and wildlife reserves are rising dramatically, often straining the environment to the limit. Inside these protected areas, grazing pressures are often just as intense, now that wild animals find it increasingly difficult to make seasonal migrations in and out of them.

Next to this baobab on Botswana's Lekhubu Island, a dead one decomposes among the rocks.

THE AFRICAN BAOBAB

Emerging life

The coat of a baobab seed is hard and water-resistant, and several hours among the acidic wastes of a baboon's digestive system will not only soften the seed coat, but also kill off any potentially damaging insects. Emerging along with an immediate supply of natural fertilizer has its advantages too. Once the seeds begin to germinate, a succession of well-spaced thunderstorms, with hot drying days in between, will help seedlings on their way.

Good years for baobab seedlings are most likely good years for other plants as well. Young baobabs may, therefore, be smothered before they get a chance to penetrate the tangle of surrounding vegetation, starved of life-giving light, water or nourishment. If they do survive among the competition in their first, most fragile months, they still need to be well watered over the next few years before they are strong enough to withstand the long dry spells that typify much of their range.

To try and add some simple science to the common sense, let me take the hypothesis of the average baobab in the previous chapter one step further. Very roughly, if 5% of the tree's annual seed crop of 30 000 eventually germinates and of those, 5% live to the following year, there will be 75 saplings. To maintain the population at existing levels, at least one of those 75 trees must survive the rigours of baobab life long enough to start reproducing.

No baobab seedling could possibly survive the attentions of so much livestock. This tree is growing in northern Tanzania.

THE AFRICAN BAOBAB

With each passing year the fast-growing tree gains strength, more resistance to drought, greater chances of surviving loss of leaves and stems to hungry goats or impala – and more flexibility to withstand trampling by cattle or Cape buffalo. Fire remains a potent danger to growing trees long after they are too big to be flattened by passing mammals. While mature baobabs are little affected by bush fires raging around their trunks, several years of saplings can be destroyed in a single blaze, particularly if grass is long and flames burn hot. Ironically, the same fire that can devastate the young baobabs may also help break the dormancy of the next crop of seeds. And, still more ironically, mature baobabs may even conduct the lightning that starts the fire that burns their offspring.

In those parts of Africa blessed with two rainy seasons, baobabs grow much faster than they do where they have to rely on a couple of consecutive months of scattered downpours. Young trees are measured by height rather than girth, and in well-watered country they may be a metre tall after two years and 10 m after 20. In areas of semi-desert, like the Sahel and southern Sudan, any trees that escape the feet and mouths of hungry livestock, as well as droughts and fires, grow much slower. Almost always, the seeds with the best chances of maturing into small trees are those that germinate on rocky hillsides, away from the attentions of grazing quadrupeds, although these saplings will only grow very slowly.

Trunks and bark

The tiny new saplings are quite unrecognizable as would-be baobabs. Instead of the finger-like leaves of mature trees, young baobabs have simple, elliptical ones, successfully concealing their identity from all but the most dedicated searcher. Saplings' leaves are paired, one opposite the other, with the next pair appearing at right angles to the ones below. As they grow, little trees produce more baobab-like leaves with three indistinct points, but these still resemble the compound, digitate foliage from which the species takes its name.

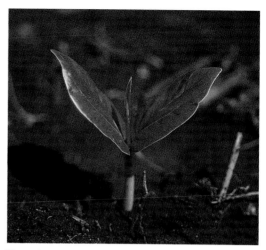

Young baobabs often go unnoticed, not least because their leaves are so different from those of mature trees.

In the first two or three years, young trees have a shrubby look, their limbs protruding horizontally. Thereafter, the branches start reaching upwards, rather than outwards, giving the tree a shape odd enough to invite a second glance. One hundred and fifty years ago Thomas Baines described young boabs in Australia as resembling a champagne bottle with a branching twig stuck in its cork. With age, baobabs of the African species begin conforming to that description too, by which time they may be designated 'pachycauls' – thick-stemmed.

Baobab trees are usually grey or grey-brown, elephant-coloured, sometimes with a red or purple tinge to them. On the mystical granite outcrop of Lekhubu Island in northern Botswana, baobabs frame the vistas over the ancient lakebed of what is now the Nxai Pan to an unbroken horizon. Some are a deep copper colour, as if chemically tainted by the alkaline soil below, others have a golden sheen to their trunks, and a few are pink on the upper surfaces of their branches, almost looking sunburnt. Not far away are the famous 'Baines Baobabs', so called because Thomas Baines made a watercolour painting of them in 1862. Struggling

Most of the trees on Lekhubu Island (left) are copper-coloured, suggesting that minerals in the soil affect the colour of their bark; however, this pink-hued tree in Namibia (right) was growing so close to others with more normal trunks, that there was no reason to think that soil composition had any effect on bark colour.

THE AFRICAN BAOBAB

to get the colours right, he notes in his diary entry for 21 May that:

'The general colour of the immense stems was grey and rough; but where the old bark had peeled and curled off, the new (of that peculiar metallic coppery-looking red and yellow which Dr. Livingstone was wont so strenuously to object to in my pictures) shone through over large portions, giving them, according to light or shade, a red or yellow grey or a deep purple tone.'

Baobab bark can be smooth and shiny, endowing trees with a lustrous aura of good health. Comparisons to human skin and the body it encases are inescapable. The surface of old trees becomes crinkled and wrinkled, or pitted with arboreal scars. Sometimes the woody matter is bunched like dripping candle wax or rolls of fat, branches splaying out to resemble waving arms. Trunks are often covered with nodules, dense enough to remind one of the knobbly stems of the baobab's Brazilian bombax relative. The bark can have the matt look of stone, too, and when bits of trunk spread over slabs of rock, it may require touch to distinguish one from the other.

Just below the outer bark is a layer of bright green, easily exposed by scratching with fingernails. This is chlorophyll, thought to help the tree photosynthesize during long leafless periods, without losing water.

Thomas Baines' sketch of baobabs that still bear his name 150 years later.

LIFE AND DEATH

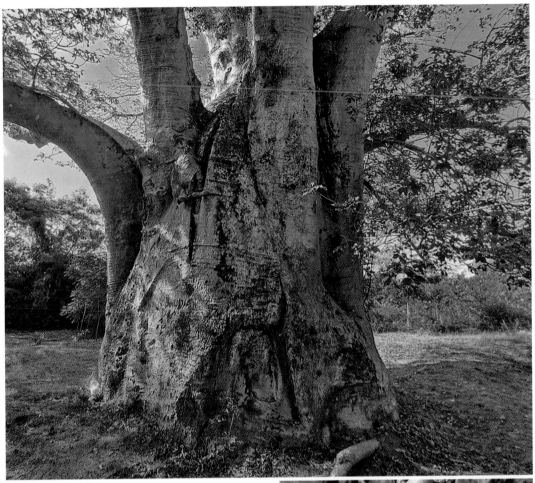

Above: The bark has grown back to close up the entrance to this tree trunk, which once sheltered an early Kenyan freedom fighter. **Right:** *Commiphora* species are leafless for most of the year and so photosynthesize through their trunks, as baobabs are also thought to do.

Species of the *Commiphora* genus can probably also absorb solar energy through their trunks and branches, vividly coloured in different shades of bright green or blue beneath the peeling, papery bark. Young fever trees (*Acacia xanthophloea*) are also often far greener-trunked than the typical yellow of their later years.

Injured trees usually heal when bark from the wound edges grows inwards to cover the bare patches, just as cuts on human skin mend. Baobab bark is remarkable for its spectacular ability to regenerate directly out of the wood of the tree, although early scars linger into later life. Such resilience is one of the reasons why the trees are able to survive such massive damage to bark and wood by thirsty, mineral-hungry elephants. These regenerative powers also have a profound effect on the tree's physiognomy. They allow trunks and branches to bend, crack and splinter, the wounds then healing so completely that the tree looks as if the contorted shape actually results from natural growth rather than well-mended injury.

On the south bank of Kenya's Sabaki River estuary, is a large hollow baobab with faint scarring of what had clearly been a square entrance-hole down at its base. It is said that this opening was cut out of the tree in 1913 by the supporters of Mekatilili Wa Menza, one of Kenya's earliest independence activists, to create a hiding place for her as she tried to evade the British authorities. Imprisoned at least twice, this ferocious leader had rallied the local Giriama people against their colonizing overlords. By all accounts, to escape capture she took refuge in the hollow trunk of this riverside tree. When I visited in 2022, the human-made hole in the tree's trunk had completely grown over, and if there was now nothing more than an indistinct outline of where it had once been, Mekatilili's reputation is wonderfully embellished with every telling of the story.

Leaves and water

On the twig ends are digitate leaves, usually five-, but sometimes four-, six- or seven-fingered (with leaves of all counts even growing on the same branch). The baobab in full foliage is a splendid sight, towering high and dark above the surrounding vegetation. The stark silhouette of the dry months is softened by the luxuriant mass of greenery.

This magnificent canopy boosts the opportunities for photosynthesis, as baobabs present hundreds of thousands of broad, chlorophyll-laden blades to the sun, and, with the aid of this solar energy, turn huge amounts of carbon dioxide and water into sugar and oxygen. Like most trees growing out in the open, rather than in dense forest, baobabs have rounded hemispherical crowns that maximize the trees' exposure to sunlight and minimize the shading of one layer of leaves by another. The digitate configuration of the leaves also lets sunlight filter in between the leaflets.

The price for such massive photosynthetic activity, however, is colossal loss of water through transpiration. The undersides of leaves are covered in holes (stomata), through which carbon dioxide is absorbed, and oxygen and water emitted. Leaves of mature baobabs are far larger than those of most trees growing in the dry African bush, and so allow the loss of much more water than do the leaves of those other trees.

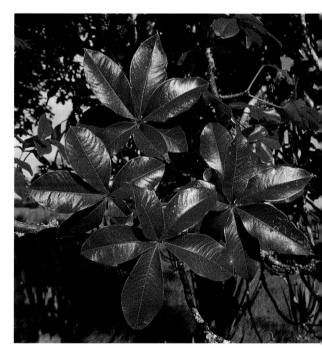

Despite the species name, *digitata*, six or seven, rather than five, leaflets often make up a single leaf.

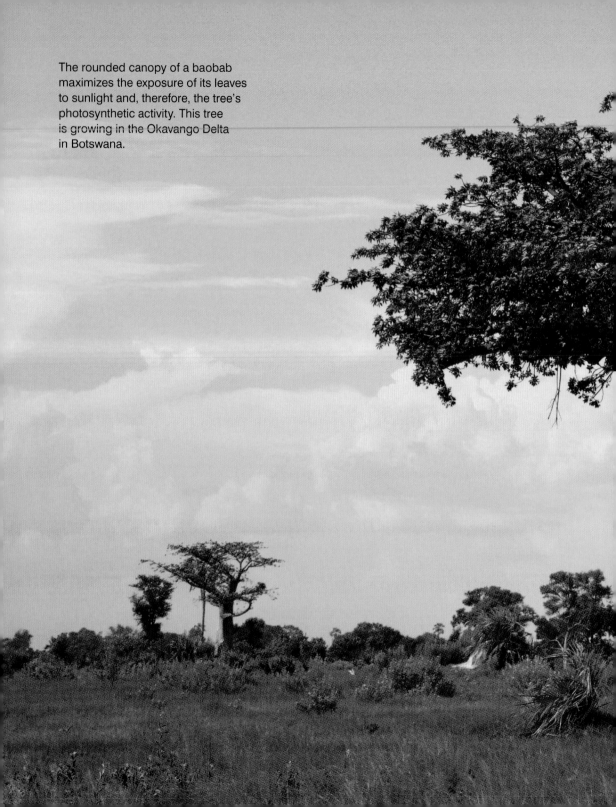

The rounded canopy of a baobab maximizes the exposure of its leaves to sunlight and, therefore, the tree's photosynthetic activity. This tree is growing in the Okavango Delta in Botswana.

Being in leaf during the rainy season gives baobabs the best chance to replenish water lost in transpiration by continually drawing up more through their roots. To minimize water loss, baobabs have an annual cycle that has them in full leaf for about four months before the tree starts absorbing nutrients from its own leaves. As it does, the green chlorophyll, which masked other pigments, begins to disappear, and carotene and xanthophyll dominate the leaf colour with oranges and yellows. When the leaflets start falling, they are finally tinged a lingering autumnal brown by the tannin.

Besides keeping their leaves for such a short time, baobabs have evolved another aid to survival – they store huge amounts of water in their wood. This high water content is not immediately obvious, and certainly doesn't make the tree any softer to the touch. Yet for all its unyielding rigidity, there is enough water in the wood to provoke debate on whether the baobab actually qualifies as a succulent.

A question of succulence

In Volume 36 of the *Cactus and Succulent Journal of Great Britain* (1974), Len Newton, then Professor of Botany at Nairobi University, posited the question 'Is the Baobab Tree Succulent?', concluding that 'it depends on what you mean by succulent'! In the absence of a universally accepted definition of a succulent this actually seems a logical, if unsatisfactory, end to the argument. Bruce Hargreaves of Botswana's National Museum defined succulents in the broadest terms as 'plants which store water' and so had no hesitation in including *Adansonia digitata* in *The Succulents of Botswana*. Plants can store water in trunks as well as leaves, and if stem-succulents are accepted into the lists, baobabs are inescapably due for inclusion. Their trunks are water-laden in the extreme, even without a fleshy consistency, as are those of desert roses (*Adenium obesum*) and the extraordinary caudiciform plants like *Pyrenacantha malvifolia*, which use their grossly swollen stems as food and water stores. Those arguing that baobabs

Top and opposite: Both baobabs and desert roses store water in their trunks, and both are often in flower when nothing else is. **Above:** *Pyrenacantha malvifolia* is perhaps the ultimate in succulent plants, with its gigantic caudex out of which grow spindly stems.

are succulents will also be comforted by their appearance in both the three-volume *Handbook of Succulent Plants* by Hermann Jacobson of Kiel Botanical Gardens, and in B P Barkhuizen's *Succulents of Southern Africa*.

Water content is best measured by comparing the weight of recently cut timber against that of air-dried wood. Freshly felled baobab trunks weigh around 840 kg per cubic metre – although clearly weight changes with the season. Air drying, when most water is extracted from the wood, brings this down to around 200 kg per cubic metre. These figures make baobabs only slightly more watery than human beings, but much less so than saguaro cacti (*Carnegiea gigantea*) of Hollywood horizons and the Arizona desert, which are 90% water after a good storm. These are the largest cacti on Earth, their flowers only blooming for 24 hours and also, incidentally, pollinated by bats at night, and birds and insects in the daytime. Like baobabs, these succulents have a far-reaching web of shallow roots to maximize absorption of moisture, but unlike baobabs they have no leaves through which to lose water, photosynthesizing entirely through their stems.

Baobabs actually rely on water to keep them upright. The liquid creates the hydraulic pressure that maintains the trees in their distended, water-logged state. Saguaro cacti store water as a jelly in their tissue. Although they can lose up to 80% of this moisture, thick waxy skin acts as a sort of supporting exoskeleton while also preventing complete dehydration. Baobabs' water loss is less extreme, but during very dry times their girths can still contract.

For such a prodigious hydraulic intake, a baobab needs an extensive web of roots. The tree's first major root in life is a tap root that heads straight down into the soil, before ballooning out just below the surface as the trunk begins expanding. When baobabs fall over,

Top: The saguaro is one of the largest cactus species on earth and, comprising almost 90% water, it is even more succulent than the baobab. **Above:** This baobab is being transplanted and shows the thick tap root that young trees soon develop.

THE AFRICAN BAOBAB

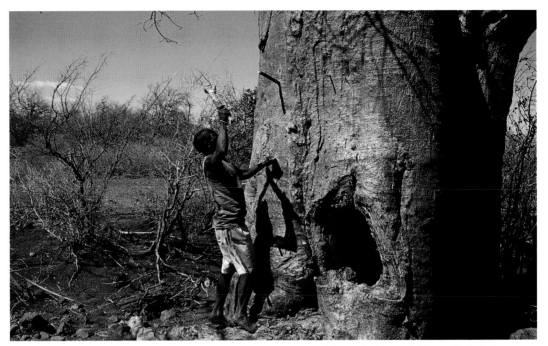

Hardwood pegs are easy to hammer into the soft, water-laden tissue of the baobab's trunk. Here a Hadzabe honey hunter makes a ladder up a tree.

this bulbous mass of solid root wood may be pulled out of the ground by the weight of the trunk, leaving a deep wide hole, like a tooth extracted from its gum. An older tree's root mass may start rotting at the same time as the heartwood in the trunk, and the tree gradually hollows both above and below the ground.

A baobab's root system is usually far closer to the surface than popularly supposed. The exposed silhouette of roots and tree may be compared to that of a wine glass, with the roots forming the flat base to the stem of the trunk. Huge baobab roots are often partly exposed above the ground, either because they are spreading out over rocks or because the soil that once covered them has eroded. One of the roots of Chapman's Baobab showed above the soil an impressive 65 m from the trunk, as thick as a bloated python.

With such enormous trunks, and often having to gather a year's supply of water from occasional storms within a few weeks, the web of a baobab's roots spreads far wider than that of many other trees. In Senegal, Michel Adanson not only measured the circumference of the trees, but also examined the roots:

'... my guide led me to a second,
which was sixty-three feet in
circumference, ... and one
of its roots, which had been
for the most part laid bare by
a neighbouring river, was a
hundred and ten feet in length,
without reckoning the part that
lay hid under the water, and
which I could not uncover.'

Various attempts have been made to devise formulae to calculate the span of baobab roots – two or three times the radius of the branches or so many times the height of the tree. In the course of my researches I explored the root systems of many baobabs and, if forced to devise a formula for root length, it would be just under three times tree height. Generally however, baobab bulk and thus water requirement is related less to height than to girth; this would therefore seem a more appropriate measurement with which to link root length.

The high water content of their wood has contrary consequences for baobabs. Elephants attack them mercilessly in times of drought, obtaining water or minerals by gouging wood out of the trunk to the point of its collapse. Yet this same waterlogged state makes the wood very difficult to burn, and saves trees from much human destruction. It also makes them extremely awkward to fell and, as if hacking down a huge tree with an axe was not work enough, a family I met on the Kenyan coast, who had cut a tree down to make space for a new house, still had to slice the felled trunk into metre-wide segments to enable its removal.

Above: There may be few baobabs in this part of Tanzania, which makes each tree more of a focal point for elephants. **Right:** This tree is defying both gravity and nature as it remains upright in such a fragile state.

THE AFRICAN BAOBAB

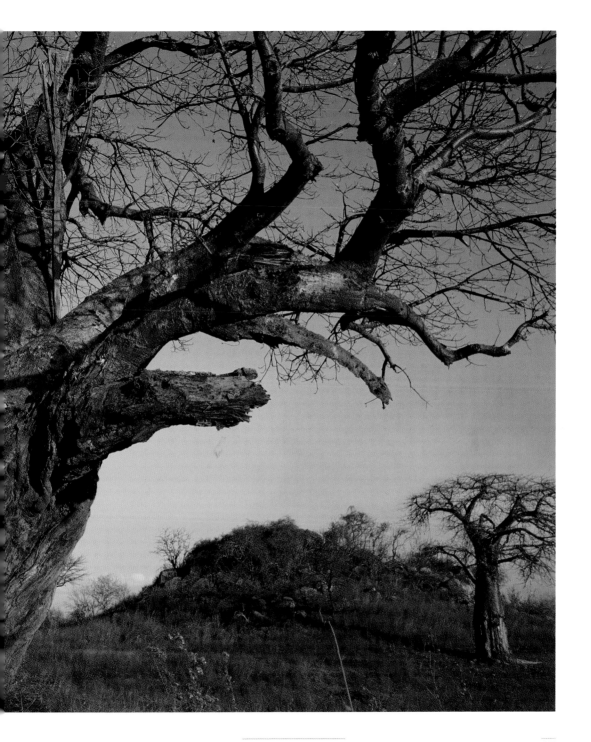

LIFE AND DEATH

A distinctive outline

The core, the character, the very essence of the baobab is its shape, size and silhouette. Baobabs need thick twigs to support large heavy leaves, giving branch ends the stumpy look of fingers clawing at the sky, as if these terminal twigs had suddenly stopped short of further bifurcations. The branches of species with smaller leaves divide into much more spindly twigs, giving such trees a much fuzzier look from a distance.

The combination of trunk and branches confers on each baobab its own distinctive outline as if each tree had its own life story to tell. One characteristic of almost all very large baobabs is that they comprise two or more boles. Sometimes these remain almost as one, encased by the same bark and probably functioning as a single part of the tree. Other boles split away from each other, so close to the ground that they could almost have emerged from different seeds. Carbon dating different trunks of the same tree has shown that these have often emerged at significantly different times from each other, although the second trunk on the tiny tree in my Nairobi garden probably sprouted ten years after planting as a result of insect damage at the top of the tap root.

Some trees retain a bottle shape from immaturity through to old age. The trunk fills out, developing either a long central tapering top, or otherwise a cluster of waving arm-like branches. Others may not fatten out to the same extent, but still produce branches continuing straight up out of the trunk, as if the tree had been pollarded and the limbs were growing again. More often, at least some branches grow out sideways and, if the tree lives long enough, these begin to sag under the twin burdens of annual crops of heavy fruit and their own water-laden weight.

As they fatten and contort, trunks and roots may clasp large rocks, which are eventually lifted off the ground.

THE AFRICAN BAOBAB

Trunks and branches may dip so low they touch the ground. One of the trunks of the famous Dorsland Tree, near Tsumkwe in Namibia, seemed to have succumbed under the burden of its own history, and all else it has carried over the past several hundred years. Bending down to the ground, the relief of no longer having to support itself seemed to have given it a new life of its own, and when we visited, tangles of young branches were thrusting their way skywards once more.

It is wrong to invest these different forms with too much significance, in that seldom do trees in a particular area show any similarities in profile. There seems little, if any, correlation between tree shape and distribution. Rather, the myriad variation in the configuration of trunks and branches is yet another aspect of what makes the trees so intriguing, non-conformist, and individual. A tree's final shape can also be affected by incidents in early life. Having the leafy top munched off by a hungry elephant, as a sapling, will almost certainly influence the outline of the mature baobab, as will the unwanted attentions of the larvae of longhorn beetles (Cerambycidae), boring their way around inside the stems.

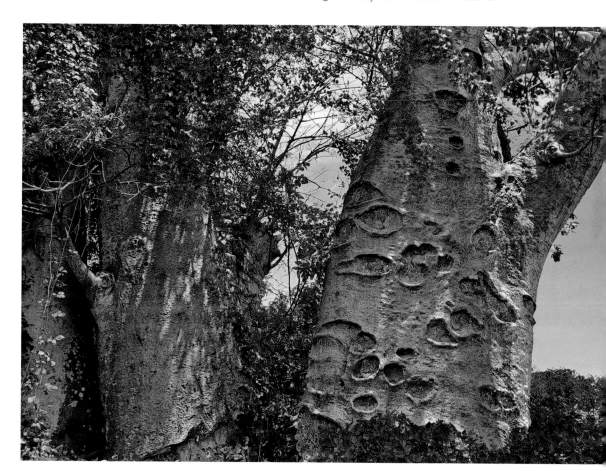

Whether or not these trunks grew from the same seed, the bark of only the larger one is badly pockmarked. The reason for this scarring is unclear.

Elephant damage to older trees provides a wonderful glimpse into the otherwise hidden secrets of a baobab's trunk, and an early chance to see if it is hollow. Aged trees of many species hollow out long before they die, but living longer, and with their wood containing so much water, baobabs are particularly inclined to do so. This seems to cause no immediate ill effects and when a big tree falls, it is actually quite a surprise to find it completely intact.

Death

Trees lengthen by growing new wood onto the tips of their branches, and they widen by adding layers around their trunks. (Carved initials or pruning scars stay in roughly the same place on a tree all its life, but initials become increasingly hard to decipher.) As old layers are buried by one new one after another, they are gradually relegated from live, functioning sapwood, to solid, yet redundant, heartwood. Gums and resins often give heartwood a different texture or colour. Being dead and contributing nothing to the workings of the tree, heartwood's principal function might seem one of structural support. Yet this slowly decaying centre may also provide the tree with a vital source of food, prolonging life by hundreds more years. New feeder roots may even grow down to suck out goodness from the rotting balloon of root material below a disintegrating trunk.

Branches often break off baobabs in their prime, the mass of fruit- or leaf-laden, waterlogged wood finally succumbing to the forces of gravity. Sometimes a single broken branch or trunk leaves others unsupported and they soon follow it earthwards, the whole finally resembling a gigantic half-peeled, half-eaten banana.

Eventually the stress of maintaining such a huge trunk, hollow or not, and all its branches, will prove too much for the root system. Disease, like the fungal affliction called sooty baobab disease, which appears in different populations from time to time, may then further weaken already fragile

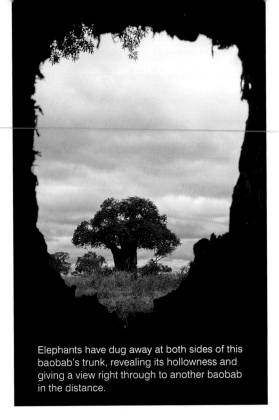

Elephants have dug away at both sides of this baobab's trunk, revealing its hollowness and giving a view right through to another baobab in the distance.

trees. Otherwise, drought takes its toll, perhaps compounded by moisture loss from the soil as surrounding ground cover is overgrazed. Weakened trees that have previously withstood frequent frosts succumb to temperatures no lower than they have endured for hundreds of years before.

Exactly how a tree collapses depends very much on its shape. Bottle-shaped trees with thick trunks and much thinner branches are more likely to lose those branches than to fall over. On more cylindrical trees, branches spreading horizontally away from the trunk may snap off, or their weight eventually exert so much leverage on the trunk that roots no longer provide a strong enough anchor to keep it on the ground.

The trunks of multi-stemmed trees usually fall one by one over a period of months or sometimes years, and it was unusual for all those of Chapman's Baobab to collapse almost in unison in January 2016.

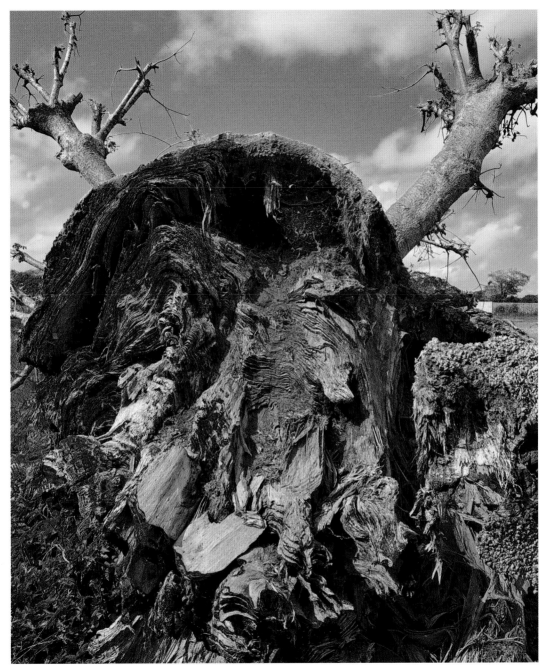

This tree left most of its roots in the ground when it collapsed, revealing that it had not yet begun to hollow out. It shows traces of growth rings.

Several months before the picture was taken, this baobab was uprooted from the ground with a view to exporting it from Kenya and replanting it on the coast of the Black Sea. The wood's high water content means that shoots continue to emerge from the trunk for many months thereafter, giving a misleading impression of the tree's wellbeing.

Trunks clearly provide a mutual support system to one another; how and when they fall depends on the architecture of the entire tree and particularly the extent to which the different trunks are fused together.

Toppling over does not always signal the death of the tree, or of a single fallen trunk. That same elasticity, derived from its waterlogged wood, makes roots bend rather than snap, and, as with the Dorsland Baobab, many near-horizontal trunks retain at least some contact with their source of nutrients and water. New shoots often sprout out of these fallen trees, like independent bushes. Round the bottom of the upended trunk, an outer layer of protective cambium may grow over the jagged fractures of snapped roots, just as it seals off scars of broken branches.

Baobabs are known to live for many more years in a supine state. Among the many reasons for the notoriety of the Baines' Baobabs in Botswana can be added the resilience of one sleeping giant.

In his diary entry Baines describes how:

*'A long circuit brought me …
to the clump of baobabs we
had seen yesterday from the
wagon; five full-sized trees
and two or three younger ones
were standing, so that when
in leaf their foliage must form
one magnificent shade. One
gigantic trunk had fallen and
lay prostrate, but still losing
none if its vitality, sent forth
branches and young leaves
like the rest.'*

THE AFRICAN BAOBAB

Trees are sometimes said to be set alight spontaneously by both breaking branches or collapsing trunks. Yet such stories always seem to be at least second-hand, and eyewitness accounts of these bizarre incidents are conspicuously lacking. Hollow baobabs are often blackened as a result of fires that were lit inside their trunks when they served as homes or hideouts while the trees were still alive. Charred stumps of broken branches are sometimes signs that honey gatherers have been at work on bees' nests. These fire scars from the tree's earlier life could be wrongly attributed to its time of collapse. Once a large baobab trunk has fallen over or crumpled where it stands, the great mass of rotting, water-laden wood may easily start to smoulder and steam. Any of these scenarios could stir minds into fitting facts to the fancy of the myth rather than to a more prosaic reality.

Even when the last root snaps, and all contact with the ground has gone, there remains enough water in the bloated stem to fuel a few hopeful shoots for a few months. But the giant dehydrates quickly and begins crumbling where it lies, the heartwood so soft and damp one can pull off chunks or push fingers into it. Eventually, the whole baobab rots away, back into the ground from which it emerged. Perhaps among the richer vegetation that is nourished by the remains of the old tree is a young one, no longer held back by the towering presence of its parent and now able to gather nutrients from the fallen corpse.

With mountains eroding and lakes silting up, why should ancient baobabs

This family in Mtwara, southern Tanzania, was nearly crushed by the collapse of a baobab. They described it falling slowly earthwards early one evening 'as if [it was] sleeping'.

not assume the distinction of near-permanent fixtures? In one of the agreements, signed in 1900, whereby Britain and Germany recognized their respective spheres of influence, baobabs were considered enduring enough features of the landscape to demarcate the Kenya–Tanganyika border:

> 'From this point the boundary follows N 70 E (astronomical) in a straight line to point No 5 (large baobab tree on the high part of the bank). On this line several mangrove poles have been planted … On the high bank the boundary goes from the baobab at No 5 past a second baobab to a third baobab. Two blocks of cement have been placed in the intervening space, and marks have been cut upon the baobabs. From the third baobab …'

Yet the baobabs disappointed. By 1993, less than a century later, no trace of any of them remained.

Top right: This collapsed baobab had been used as a shelter. **Middle right:** Three huge trunks have collapsed in different directions; within a few years, the only sign that a baobab ever grew here will be relict clumps of invasive vegetation. **Bottom right:** This is the scar left after the first of two trunks collapsed; how long the unsupported survivor will stay standing remains to be seen. **Opposite:** The fallen tree that so intrigued Baines 150 years ago is still sending out shoots every year.

THE AFRICAN BAOBAB

Despite having fallen over, this baobab's root system is clearly intact and is sending water and nutrients up to the three healthy new shoots.

CHAPTER FIVE

How old? How big?

Big baobabs must be old. Can anything grow that huge without taking hundreds, if not thousands, of years to do so? However efficiently their root systems collect water, and no matter what devices they have evolved to limit moisture loss through leaves, given where they grow, big trees must be old trees. That is the voice of good sense, and the most profound science is not going to silence it. Small is certainly not necessarily young in the tree world, but big simply has to be old.

The massive bulk of Chapman's Baobab in Botswana once beckoned travellers from far away. It was both camped under and measured by the explorers James Chapman, Thomas Baines and David Livingstone, and many others before its collapse in 2016.

THE AFRICAN BAOBAB

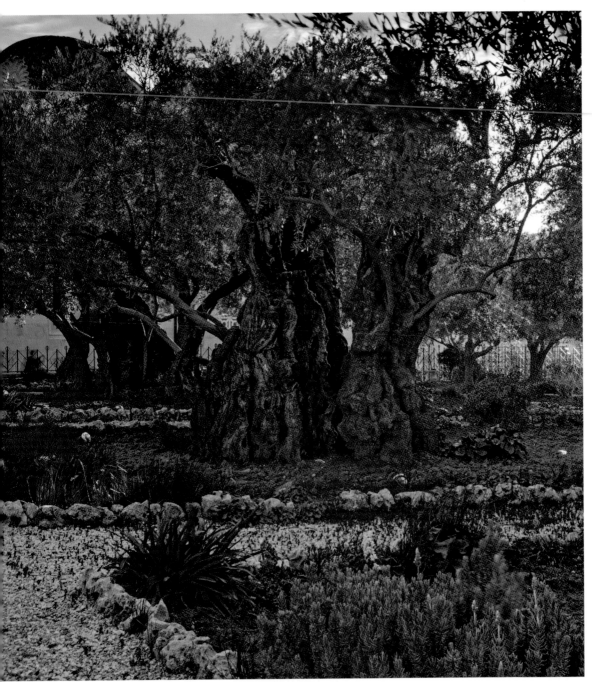

Did this olive tree in Gethsemane actually witness Jesus Christ's last prayers before his arrest and crucifixion?

THE AFRICAN BAOBAB

Ageing trees

And how old is old? Almost anyone with at least a passing interest in baobabs asks the question. The Prussian explorer Friedrich von Humboldt may only just have been exaggerating in calling baobabs the 'oldest organic monuments of our planet' and suggesting they 'would date back to the times of the Pyramid builders' (c. 2 500 BC).

Two hundred years ago, Von Humboldt, and other travellers with more fanciful than scientific bents, could make such unfounded assertions without challenge. Today, in the times of written history scattered with dates, chronologies and anniversaries, 'old' has become an increasingly inadequate description of either natural or artificial monuments. The age of everything, from the universe onwards, is questioned, investigated and, if possible, ascertained.

Knowing a tree's age does satisfy a certain curiosity, and perhaps enhances the sense of awe and wonder one feels in its presence. It also slots trees into a historical perspective, as witnesses to passing generations. Yet at the same time, answering the 'How old?' question inevitably risks demystifying these ancient relics. Some may be content just to wonder if Jesus Christ actually prayed under the olive trees (*Olea europaea*) still growing in what is left of the Garden of Gethsemane, or if there remains an oak in Sherwood Forest that sheltered Robin Hood and his Maid Marion. And could the baobabs at Malindi, on the Kenyan coast, be the very same ones that astounded Vasco da Gama?

Ageing ancient trees remains a combination of science, practical good sense, guesswork and wishful thinking. Science's contribution comes largely from carbon dating which, with ever-improving technology, is the best way of ascertaining the age of any organic material. Radiocarbon (principally carbon-14) in molecules of carbon dioxide is continually absorbed by green plants from the atmosphere. Once a plant dies, the process ceases, and the accumulated radiocarbon

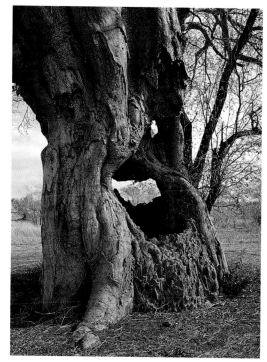

Because most old baobabs are hollow, it is not possible to determine their age either by carbon-dating original wood or by counting rings.

steadily declines. The rate of decline is expressed in terms of a half-life – the length of time that half the amount of radiocarbon takes to disappear. The graph of radiocarbon decline is the same for any organism, so date of death can be estimated by assessing the amount of carbon remaining at the time of measurement.

Heartwood, from the centre of a tree, is in all respects dead, and samples from standing trees for carbon dating can usually be extracted by screwing in an increment borer with a T-shaped handle. This technique relies on the presence of 'original' material in the tree to date and is less suitable for older hollow baobabs. Even solid baobabs are often so huge that extracting a sample of wood from the middle of a standing tree would need a borer far bigger and stronger than any produced thus far.

There is a timeless serenity about any
big baobab at the end of the day.

The research of E R Swart was published in the 18 May 1963 issue of *Nature*. It focused on the results of carbon dating the wood of a baobab felled during the bush-clearing operations before the Zambezi River backed up behind Kariba Dam in Zimbabwe. The tree had a radius of 2.28 m, and wood samples were taken from its centre and from halfway between the centre and the outside. The centre sample was calculated to be 1 010 years old and that from midway 740 (each plus or minus 100 years).

At the time of writing, significant radiocarbon dating work is being undertaken by Adrian Patrut of Babes-Bolyai University in Romania. Of several papers on the age of baobabs, the 2018 paper entitled 'The Demise of the Largest and Oldest African Baobabs', and of which Patrut is the main author, summarizes the estimated ages of 15 of these monumental trees, established by extracting small samples of wood remains from the hollow cavities in the trunks. At the same time as disclosing the estimated ages of each tree, the paper recorded how the trees collapsed and postulated reasons why so many of them had died in the preceding decade.

The oldest specimen was the Panke Baobab in Zimbabwe, estimated to be about 2 500 years old before it died c. 2010–2011, with the Dorsland Tree the second oldest at 2 100. Some of the 15, like James Chapman's, had completely collapsed, while on other trees, one or more of their main trunks had fallen away. So many huge trees dying within a few years of each other is more than mere coincidence, but it seems difficult to attribute any specific cause other than possible drought, which would particularly affect trees already reduced to a fragile state through age.

The Dorsland Tree may be the oldest baobab in Namibia and over 130 years of history are etched into its bark.

THE AFRICAN BAOBAB

In temperate climes, where years divide into definite seasons of growth and rest, counting annual rings is generally an accurate way of calculating tree ages. Rings show as concentric circles of light and dark wood, the large and light-coloured cells of spring and early summer growth contrasting with the darker, denser ones of autumn and winter. Nearer the equator temperatures vary less, but baobab habitat is usually characterized by distinct rainy seasons, and rings certainly show on felled or fallen baobabs, especially once the trunk dries out and the wood starts to crack. (Actually, for baobabs, 'rings' is a misleading description, as more often one is trying to read parallel curved lines rather than concentric circles.) These rings probably indicate wet periods after dry, and whether they are annual or not depends on the seasonality of the climate. In parts of Africa with one distinct rainy season, rings may work out to be laid down yearly – droughts excepted. Baobabs growing furthest from the equator are most likely to show their ages in this way, particularly in southern Africa or Sudan, where hot and usually wet summers contrast with colder and rainless winters.

So, where does all this take us when it comes to discovering the age of *Adansonia digitata*? Often hollow, and with ill-defined rings, which may or may not be annual, it is a poor candidate for scientific dating. Even allowing for such rings as there are to be annual ones, the huge, gnarled trunks of old baobabs are virtually impossible to saw through, and much too thick and twisted for complete samples to be extracted from their timber.

Michel Adanson made the first serious attempt to age baobabs. In 1749 he came across two on the Magdalene Islands off Cape Verde, one of which he estimated to be 5 150 years old. A hundred years later, Adanson's record found itself under attack by Livingstone, whose scientific bent was severely constrained by a dogmatic belief in the Creation theories of Bishop James Ussher. By counting the ages of Adam's descendants, as described in the Book of Genesis, and overlaying these on

Rings – or even slices – in baobab wood are often clearly visible when a tree has been cut or has fallen down. If there is only one rainy season per year where the tree is growing, these rings may be annual, but the unpredictability of the African climate makes them an unreliable indicator of age.

known dates of historic events in his chronology, *The Annals of the World*, the bishop fixed the date of the world's creation at 23 October 4004 BC. The bishop went on to declare that the Ark touched down on Mount Ararat on 5 May 2348 BC. Anyone adhering rigidly to his timetable had to conclude that Adanson was proposing the 5 000-year-old tree would have been alive before the Great Flood. And no tree could have survived the Great Flood. Adanson must have been wrong, or, even worse, was inferring the Flood was a fairy tale. In *Missionary Travels*, David Livingstone, with a surprising touch of jingoism, writes that the baobab:

> '… is the same as those which Adanson and others believed, from specimens seen in Western Africa, to have been alive before the flood. Arguing with a peculiar mental idiosyncracy resembling colour-blindness, common among the French of the time, these savans came to the conclusion that 'therefore there never was any flood'. I would back a true mowana [baobab] against a dozen floods, provided you do not boil it in hot sea-water; but I cannot believe that any of those now alive had a chance of being subjected to the experiment of even the Noachian deluge.'

Ironically perhaps, the oldest tree species in the world are not necessarily growing in the latitudes between the tropics. Continual warmth and frequent rain might seem to create an ideal environment for trees to live long lives, but in fact these conditions are generally better suited to fast growth; and growing fast and living long are, to some extent, mutually exclusive.

It is not easy to determine the longest-lived species of tree and there are a number of contenders. The line-up can be further confused by introducing trees that are growing out of truly ancient rootstock but are themselves of no great age. The dark, poisonous, red-berried yew (*Taxus baccata*) is one of these. Found all over Europe, east to the Himalayas and south into North Africa, some yews are almost certainly at least fuelled by rootstock well over 5 000 years old, even if the trees themselves are nowhere near this age.

The Great Basin bristlecone pine (*Pinus longaeva*) is the other likely contender. The venerable specimen known as the Methuselah Tree has been carbon dated at 4 800 years old, and whole clumps of trees seem to be over 4 000 years of age. With half a year of night-time frosts and lots of snow, the pale, stony slopes of California's White Mountains provide an unlikely homeland for such ancient trees. Icy winds blast the mountains, rainfall is scant, and, like baobabs, the pines collect whatever water they can with a far-reaching network of near-surface roots.

Another possible challenger for the oldest tree title has been recently identified as a particular specimen of Patagonia cypress (*Fitzroya cupressoides*) growing in the Chilean Andes and known locally as El Gran Abuelo – the Grandfather Tree. Researchers extracted almost 2 500 years' worth of rings from the venerable 'Grandfather' with an increment borer, but their equipment could not reach the middle of the tree, so they had to devise a formula to calculate the number of rings in the inaccessible heart of the tree. Their final estimate was an age of 5 400 years. Fellow dendrologists await the publication of their findings and reasoning in a reputable scientific journal.

In fine testimony to the diversity of California's landscape, north of the White Mountains and

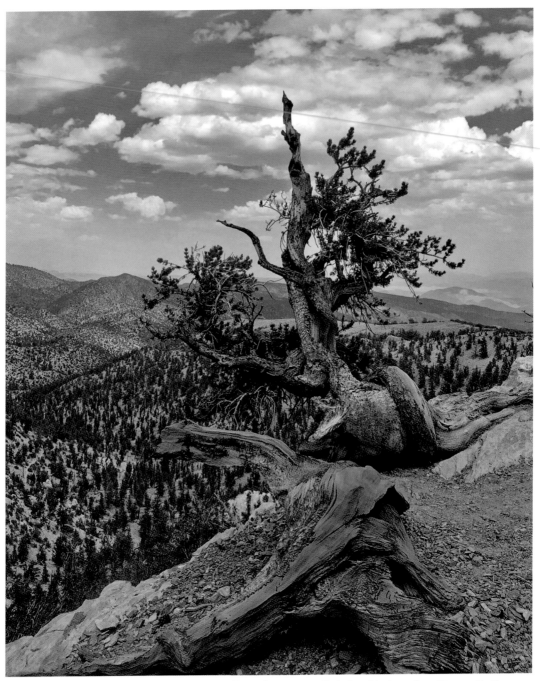

The stunted bristlecone pines of California's White Mountains are most likely the oldest species of tree on Earth.

THE AFRICAN BAOBAB

closer to the sea is the ancestral land of the ancient species of coastal and giant redwoods (*Sequoia sempervirens* and *Sequoiadendron giganteum*, respectively) the latter known in Britain, where they grow very easily, as *Wellingtonia*, in tribute to the Duke. In California, high rainfall and summer mists create ideal conditions for these towering trees, which once grew all over the Pacific Northwest before their range began shrinking under the relentless assaults of axe and saw. Enough of these trees have been cut down for many sets of rings to have been counted, and 3 200 years seems to be the oldest recorded.

Big baobabs are old, and most old specimens are big, but this does not mean that small trees are necessarily young. Access to moisture is crucial to the size of a tree whose wood is three-quarters water. The wizened baobabs on Botswana's Lekhubu Island seem to grow straight out of the rocks. Roots must find their way down between the cracks to such sandy soil as there is below, and most of whatever rain that falls drains off the slabs of stone, with little benefit to the trees. Similarly, the roots of many of the trees along the Kenyan coast spread out over a solid surface of jagged and impenetrable rock, which only allows for the collection of water and root-borne nutrition from the surface. Yet these twisted and contorted baobabs may be just as old as was the massive six-trunked bulk of Chapman's Baobab. And even big trees seem to reach a stage in later life when expansion slows, before intake of food and water becomes just enough to maintain their existing dimensions and growth is suspended altogether.

There is much evidence to show that growth rates, and so eventually size, are genetically as well as environmentally determined. A painted plaque beside the grove of baobabs at Gedi Forest Nursery on the Kenyan coast once informed visitors that the trees were planted in 1979. The grove appears to have begun with 49 seedlings, each set three yards from its neighbour, in a square of seven trees by seven. There is very little sign of position favouring

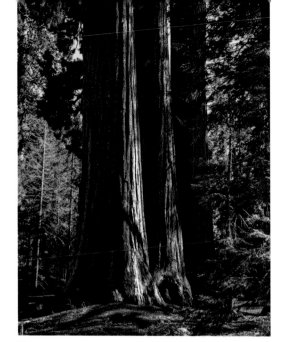

These huge giant redwoods may not be the oldest trees in North America but are easily the largest.

one tree over another, either then or now. At the end of August 2022, 38 remained of the original 49. Of these, several were over 200 cm around, measured at breast height (a scientific standard), and significantly fewer were less than 70 cm in circumference. The largest baobab, 250 cm around, was growing right next to the smallest, at 60 cm – a huge difference, although perhaps accounted for, at least to some extent, by the larger tree drawing on the smaller one's resources.

There is nothing in the Gedi records to show the origins of the seeds from which these trees emerged. One can only assume that, if they did not all come from the same pod, they were at least representative samples of seeds from around the area. What this demonstrates is not so much the rate of baobab growth – those at Gedi are very close together, given their height and age, and are depriving each other of *lebensraum*. Rather, it shows how much genetic variation, whether in growth rates or any other characteristic, there may be within a single population of trees.

When gazing at a huge and magnificent baobab, it is impossible to delink grandeur from age and to reach any conclusion other than that they must be among the most ancient trees in the world. What little scientific evidence there is to help age these trees at least supports the guesswork and conjecture, and baobabs can truly claim the title of the oldest trees in Africa, whether in terms of average age or the longevity of individual trees. They are also the fattest trees in Africa, a record rendered all the more extraordinary by the dryness of their surrounds.

Measuring a baobab

Baobab girth can be awkward to measure, the easiest method being to put a tape around the trunk. This works well during the tree's early years when baobab boles are roughly circular. Yet these trees live unpredictable existences, and their trunks twist and bend, developing indents and depressions. Big branches or new trunks shoot off from close to the ground, all making circumference measurements increasingly irregular and subjective.

A self-portrait of Thomas Baines sketching in April 1862 from the branches of a baobab tree near Lake Ngami in Botswana.

With oaks or beeches being the largest trees early European travellers had ever encountered, their first reaction on seeing an African baobab was often to estimate its girth. Measuring tapes were clearly not on most expeditions' equipment lists, leading explorers to employ confusingly disparate techniques to record a tree's dimensions. Cadamosto walked a tree 'seventeen paces round the foot' while Adanson was more scientific and:

> '. . . extended my arms, as wide
> as possible I could, thirteen
> times, before I embraced
> its circumference; and for
> greater exactness, I measured
> it afterwards round with
> packthread, and found it to be
> sixty-five feet.'

Thomas Baines explored a lot of Namibia and northern Botswana but does not appear to have accurately taped any of the trees he described or painted. On 22 July 1858, while on the fateful journey when Livingstone would accuse him of stealing stores, he 'measured' a baobab:

> '. . . equal in circumference to
> twelve times the length of my
> extended arms, which estimating
> my fathom at only five feet would
> give a measurement of sixty'.

Later, on the Northern Goldfields Expedition of 1871, during which Baines kept meticulous diaries, he found a baobab, 'ten times the span of my extended arms or, perhaps, nearly 50 feet'. From this we can at least discern that Baines's reach had not diminished in 13 years.

THE AFRICAN BAOBAB

No matter how we try and determine their age, there can be no escaping the fact that big baobabs must be old baobabs.

The tree that so astounded Chapman in 1852 had a 'circumference at the base to be twenty-nine yards'. A year later Livingstone found himself camped under the same tree 'of six branches united into one trunk. At three feet off the ground it was eighty-five feet in circumference', only two feet less than Chapman's measurement. The difference could, at least in part, be accounted for by Chapman's having been taken at ground level, or simply by dry season contraction.

Charles Sweeney describes his time in the Nuba Mountains of southern Sudan in *Background of Baobabs*. There, the average girth of 845 trees, taken about a metre off the ground, measured 7.5 m. From these and a mass of other reported measurements, it would be safe to say that 15 m is a big tree, over 20 m exceptional, and anything more than 25 m is worthy of entry in the record books.

West African trees seem to be smaller, and the largest reported from Senegal in Notes Africaines was 21 m. Swart's carbon-dated, 1 000-year-old tree was 14 m around its trunk.

Scientifically, girth is sometimes measured at ground level (GGL), occasionally at waist height (GWH), and most often at breast height (GBH), which now seems to have standardized at 1.3 m. Measurements are taken by stretching a cord around the trunk. This produces some distorted results, particularly on concave trunks or those with protruding ridges or more than one stem; however, the technique is relatively clear and easily executed, and different people measuring the same tree are likely to come up with roughly similar figures. This is more than can be said of the alternative, which has the tape contouring the trunk to take account of cracks and indentations – the *méthode des*

No matter how abundant its water supply, this baobab at Lake Manyara in Tanzania must have taken hundreds of years to grow so large.

THE AFRICAN BAOBAB

sinuosités, as *Notes Africaines* put it, against the *méthode de la corde tendue*. Figures arrived at the former way can be very subjective, as one person takes account of a particularly deep fissure in the trunk that another may ignore.

Even given a standardized measuring method, comparing the girth of the same tree at different times in its life can be misleading. Measured again in 1966, Chapman's tree was down to 80 feet in circumference. This and other similar comparisons are used to support arguments either that baobabs, particularly hollow ones, shrink with age, or that they expand and contract in wet and dry weather. Both may be true, but had elephants, perhaps, dug away at the trunk sometime during the previous 100 years, or could local people have harvested successive rings of bark for rope- or basket-making? Was erosion around the bottom of the tree enough to give recent height above the ground a noticeably lower base point? Much of the root system under the canopy of Chapman's tree had been exposed, the ground gradually worn away by the shuffling feet of generations of nomadic peoples, Tswana settlers, Chapman, Livingstone, and motor-borne visitors like me.

Big baobabs are best documented in southern Africa, with its far-reaching network of roads and long-established scientific societies. Near Modjadjiskloof in South Africa was a baobab – the Sunland or Platland tree – which the owners of the land on which the remains of it grow once described in their publicity material as the biggest in the world. Claiming a circumference of 46.8 m, their contention may well have been justified, until 2016 when the larger of two fused trunks collapsed. There is no suggestion that the existence of a bar and wine cellar within its hollow centre in any way contributed to its demise! Now, with a circumference of over 34 m, South Africa's champion baobab is almost certainly the Sagole Big Tree (pictured on pages 6 and 7), which also tops the list in the South African Dendrological Foundation's database. In the Venda language it is known as *muri kunguluwa* or 'the tree

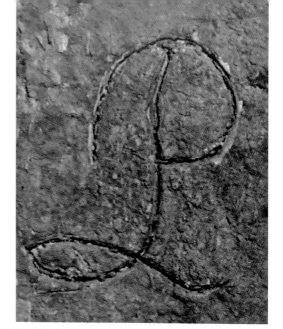

David Livingstone carved his initials inside this baobab near the mouth of the Zambezi River in 1858.

that roars' – at least in its leafy months when the wind blasts through its verdant branches.

It may seem more natural for the biggest baobabs to be growing in the heart of their range, not down at their southernmost limits. However, in northern Botswana and northeast Namibia there are vast trees, magnificent both in girth and height. Using the *méthode de la corde tendue*, I measured the Grootboom near Tsumkwe, before its collapse, at 29.5 m. Using the *méthode des sinuosites* to take account of larger indents, it came out at 32.6 m around. Even more stupendous was its height – well over 30 m – and if there was ever a search for the baobab of greatest volume, this would have been my nominee.

When all the science is said and the measuring done, knowing when a baobab first pushed its bright green shoot above the surface of the Earth is the only really accurate way to age it. The chains of human memory, which should link the past with the present, are disconcertingly fragile and, in the end, unreliable. In the African countryside trees may be remembered as having appeared the same year

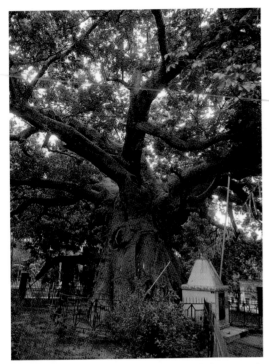

The Parijaat baobab in India's Uttar Pradesh is a sacred tree whose origins, like those of other ancient baobabs in India, are unknown.

presumably a banyan tree (*Ficus benghalensis*), but in 1575, when Moghul emperor Akhbar the Great entered the town, he found 'infidels . . . with a desire to obtain the rewards that are promised in their creed . . . casting themselves down into the deep river from the top of a high tree'. This tree has an average diameter of over 6 m and a vast mound of a trunk comprised of six stems fused together. From a distance, it could be a banyan, but it is in fact a baobab. Its survival has been threatened by recurrent Ganges floods washing away supporting soil around its roots, so to prevent further erosion, a protective concrete wall has been constructed around its base.

This Ganges tree has received the attentions of carbon daters who have estimated it to be just shy of 800 years old, which is almost the same age as a second famous Indian baobab, the Parijaat tree at Kintoor, also in Uttar Pradesh, for which the date of planting has been given as around AD 1 200. Both Indian specimens, incidentally, tolerate several days of frost most years. Like many baobabs in India, these are solitary trees, and with no other specimens nearby, locals could be forgiven for believing their tree was the only one in the world, so endowing it with particular spiritual significance.

While Africa's written historical record is only of relatively recent events, the continent has a wealth of ancient painted art on cave walls and cliff overhangs. Yet surprisingly little depicts trees and plants, even though baobabs have been vital in sustaining Africa's primates, right through to the emergence of *Homo sapiens* and beyond. If early African art was simply the product of representational skill and imagination, it seems inconceivable that the artists would not have included these trees in their paintings. Many authorities opine that much of this art represents experiences in trance-like states of altered consciousness. If the supernatural powers channelled through these artists derived from animals – particularly eland, kudu, sable and giraffe – this may go some way to explain the paucity of painted trees.

as the firstborn son of a chief, and sometimes trees were even planted to celebrate special occasions. The emergence of others may be connected to the rainstorm that relieved the worst of all droughts – events yes, but seldom dates.

Written or photographic history is relatively new to Africa and of little help in ageing things as ancient as baobab trees. The oldest written descriptions of this quintessentially African tree are curiously of a specimen outside the continent. Allahabad, known in its pre-Islamic life as Pratishthana, has always been a holy city, marked on ancient maps as the place where the Yamuna River joins the Ganges. Chinese explorer Hiuen Tsang visited this sacred confluence about AD 630 and wrote of 'a celebrated Deva Temple in front of which was a great wide-spreading umbrageous tree'. This was

THE AFRICAN BAOBAB

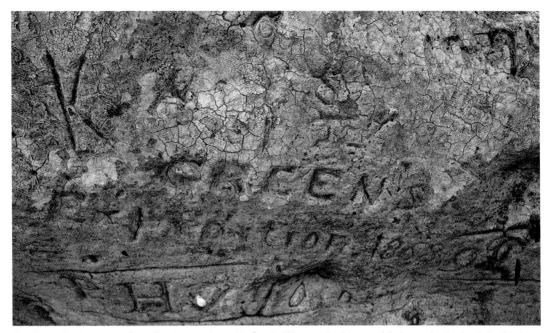

The Green brothers were Canadian hunters based in South Africa, and evidence of their passing is clearly legible in the eponymous tree – 'GREEN'S EXPEDITION 1858,9'.

If human depictions of baobabs on cave walls are inexplicably scarce, human beings have left many signs of their passing on the actual tree, sometimes etched deep enough in its trunk to last the rest of its life. Two hundred and fifty years ago, sailors arriving in strange anchorages were encouraged to leave evidence of their coming before the ships of rival colonial powers got there. Overland explorers were similarly keen to record their passing, and Livingstone is said to have etched 'DL' into the bark of both Chapman's Baobab and a tree near Victoria Falls. That he also inscribed his initials inside a hollow baobab at Shiramba, downstream of Tete and towards the mouth of the Zambezi River, seems beyond doubt once these were identified inside the trunk by explorer Quentin Keynes. In his diary entry for 16 September 1858, Livingstone gives a complete description of the tree where his initials were found and whose circumference he then measured at 72 feet around.

Further west, and ten years after Livingstone's death, Dorsland trekkers began their exodus from South Africa, escaping British colonial dominance and threats to their freedom of worship. The scattering of their historical and religious monuments clearly shows the different routes they took on the great trek up to Angola. One of these groups passed a huge baobab, now known as the Dorsland Tree, on which they carved '1883'. Not long after, realizing the only way to secure Namibia was to run it as a true colony, Germany dispatched Schutztruppe to enforce its occupation. A detachment of these troops went past the Dorsland Tree too, and at least three of them, H Gathemann, E Heller and D Hannemann, engraved their names and '1891'.

I passed by to pay my respects to the Dorsland Tree, not by ox wagon or on the back of a horse, but on four wheels. It was well over a century since the Schutztruppe's visit, and I felt an easy sense of contact with them in seeing the work of their hands exactly where they had made it. The tree had collapsed, although it was clearly still alive, its fallen trunk backed by a watery evening sun setting behind the cracked mud of a waterhole. Skinks scurried in and out of holes in its trunk, and a swallow-tailed bee-eater darted from a perch at passing insects. The few fruit that hung rather sadly from its branches seemed to imply that this giant of a tree was using most of its dwindling energies merely staying alive, and soon even doing this would take more than it had left.

Evidence that a huge tree was already enormous 100 or 200 years ago offers no help in ageing it, only in placing it in the context of human history. Recent writings, while verifying the ages of many young baobabs, make no contribution to the debate on how old is really old. No ancient African trees are set down in written records to speak their ages for the species. So, perhaps thankfully, the conjecture continues, and taxi drivers from Dakar to Dar es Salaam, Angola to Ethiopia, can continue pointing out the oldest baobab in the world. And who can prove them wrong?

In the words of W H Auden, 'knowledge may have its purpose, but guessing is always more fun than knowing'.

The sun sets behind a silhouetted baobab in Namibia, as it does every night behind thousands of other baobabs all over Africa.

THE AFRICAN BAOBAB

CHAPTER SIX

A forest in itself

'In short the whole of this calabash tree seemed to form a forest in itself', concluded Michel Adanson on first describing a baobab tree. Wherever they grow, baobabs nurture their own micro-communities of plants and animals. Some animals are casual visitors to baobabs, using them simply because they are big trees – usually the biggest ones around – and so offer the highest vantage points, the best hunting ground or the largest choice of nest sites. Other animals make use of traits such as hollowness or wrinkled bark, which these trees provide much more generously than any others do.

Despite being leafless these baobabs are home to many creatures.

THE AFRICAN BAOBAB

A Tanzanian community

In southern Tanzania, on the way from Morogoro to Iringa, the road winds down into the valley of the Great Ruaha River. The very name resonates with all that is most wild, mysterious and romantic about Africa, and the river does not disappoint. The road follows its northern bank for about 20 km as the river cuts through the northern end of the Udzungwa Mountains, creating what is locally known as Baobab Valley.

The trees stretch away from the river, grey, sometimes pinky, trunks reflecting the sunlight far up the slopes. Those growing on flatter ground closer to the road are larger, and so appear older than the smaller, more distant ones. In fact, baobabs on more level land will almost always grow much bigger, both food and water being more plentiful and easily absorbed than if they were clinging to a stony hillside.

This was July, that time of year when life in tropical Africa seems to be marking time, awaiting the press of some hidden hormonal trigger to restart it. For once, nearly all the baobabs seemed to be marching to the beat of the same biological drum, bare, scarcely a leaf, flower or fruit to be seen.

The baobabs dominated the valley's vegetation, yet they were only one part of a mosaic of trees and shrubs that covered this dried land. A tangled mass of impenetrable acacia and *Commiphora* bush, mostly bare-branched, grew like a barbed-wire fence along the roadside. A few black thorn acacias (*Acacia mellifera*) displayed their creamy white blooms on bare branches, and all over the hillsides, in among the baobabs, bright clumps of pink desert roses stood out against the rocks and desiccated vegetation.

Even in late morning, sunbirds were flitting among the baobabs, although they seemed to be using these as mere staging posts on their way to the acacia blossoms. Brown parrots flashed their green rumps in flight, and ashy starlings were visible among the bare branches or pecking around on the ground below. Crowned and Von der Decken's hornbills swooped between the trees with typically undulating flight.

Baboons were playing their daredevil games along the roadside. Were they so prolific because there was so much baobab fruit to feast on every year? Or were there so many baobabs because the baboons were doing such a good job of dispersing seeds? The answer was probably yes to both questions. There were also very few people around to persecute the monkeys, and not a lot of livestock to nibble off the tips of young trees. The inhabitants of the few small roadside settlements had preserved the baobabs around their huts, although some had that lopped look, suggesting branches were being cut so domestic animals could eat young leaves.

On the far side of the river is the protected part of the Udzungwa Mountains. There, four greater kudu picked their way down between the baobabs to the water, a male with magnificent spiralling horns, a smaller male and two lighter-coloured females. Baboons were drinking just upstream of the kudu, and downstream a crocodile feigned sleep on a sandbank.

Here was a community of which baobabs were an integral component, crucial to the continued existence of some of the other plants and animals, less important to others. Many of the different plants, which together create a community, simply share the same space. They require similar conditions, and are as likely to compete for light, water, food and space as to benefit from each other's presence. Some species may offer incidental shade, shelter or support to others, and the decaying leaves of one may nourish young of another. Yet occasionally a tree of a different species grows so close to a baobab, and looks so healthy, it seems at least one of them is actively benefitting in some way from this closeness. Black thorn acacia, desert date (*Balanites aegyptiaca*) or tamarind (*Tamarindus indica*), often flourish in the shelter of big baobabs, almost trunk to trunk, sharing resources seemingly to the detriment of neither. On the East African coast, invasive neem trees

THE AFRICAN BAOBAB

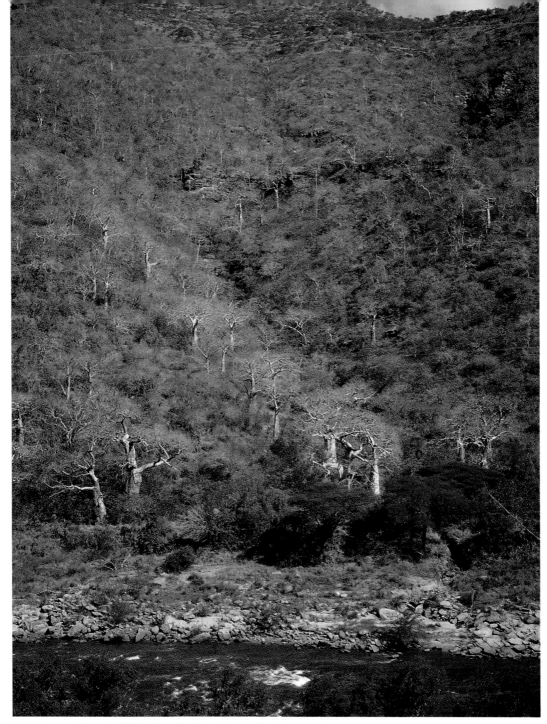

Baobabs stretch up the hillside from the Great Ruaha River in central Tanzania.

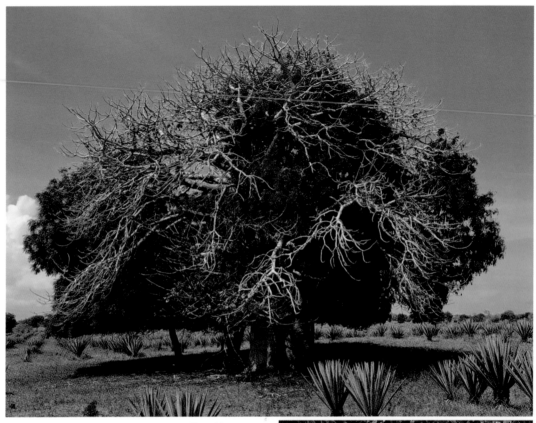

Above: Neem trees are not indigenous to East Africa, but are well suited to its climate; their seeds are easily spread by birds, who often deposit these close to baobab trunks. Both trees grow together, with the neem – as here – distinguished by its leafiness.
Right: Here, neem, baobab and fig trunks are all competing for space.

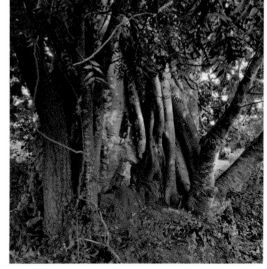

(*Azadirachta indica*) have their seeds dispersed by birds or bats, which often drop them right at the bottom of a baobab trunk, where they grow very quickly, with no obviously adverse effects on their towering neighbours. Neem are indigenous to the Indian subcontinent, but are so well established in East Africa that they have their own Swahili name, *mwarubaini*, which means '40' and refers to the number of different ailments the tree and its parts are thought to treat.

THE AFRICAN BAOBAB

Epiphytes and parasites

Some inter-plant relationships are more intimate than others. Epiphytes, like lichens and mosses, depend on their host for nothing more than a secure place to grow. Nestling snugly on the bark or in a cleft between a tree's branches, they gather sustenance from the atmosphere or from decomposing plant matter that collects around their roots. Being so smooth-barked, the flat upper surfaces of baobab branches seldom offer epiphytes good rootholds, but the cracks, folds and forks in the tree make ideal sheltered refuges where seeds germinate easily and growth can continue undisturbed. Many orchids are epiphytic, growing in clumps on big branches or in clefts between the limbs of a tree. As a whole, African members of the Orchidaceae family prefer cool, damp environments, but a few species are suited to the warmth of baobab territory.

Passive lodgers though epiphytes may be, some cause the death of their host as certainly as any parasite would. A violet-backed starling or orange-bellied parrot flies away from a fruiting fig tree and deposits its seed-laden droppings in the fork of a nearby baobab. This simple act may sentence the baobab to death as effectively as the first cut of an axe – although it may be 100 years or more before the tree finally sheds its last leaf.

Figs

Ficus is a large genus, whose best-known species are probably the multiple-trunked banyan tree (*Ficus benghalensis*) and the sacred bodhi fig (*Ficus religiosa*), both endemic to the Asian subcontinent. Figs are also strongly represented in Africa, where many of the species are epiphytic. 'Strangler fig' describes those figs starting life in the fork of a mature tree (as does the banyan), which they eventually kill. Once seeds have germinated, and the seedlings are well settled on their host, the stranglers send down aerial roots. These claw their way to the ground, where they take hold and begin channelling water and minerals to the leaves and branches. What was a root slowly starts to function as a trunk.

Top: Leopard orchids (*Ansellia africana*) are distributed from sea level to well above the altitudinal limit for baobabs, and clumps of this epiphyte are sometimes seen festooning the silhouettes of these trees.
Above: Although orchids typically prefer cool, damp climates, this one (*Angraecum* sp.) is growing on the trunk of a baobab at Gedi on the Kenyan coast.

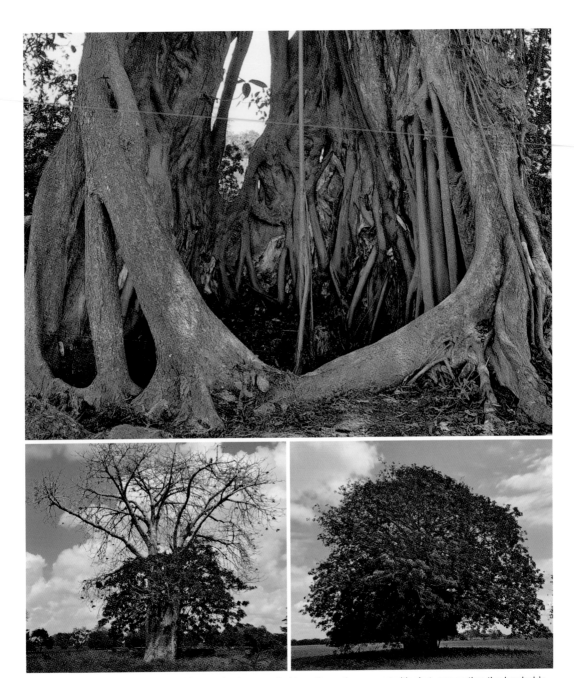

Top: Here a baobab once grew, until it was slowly strangled by a fig, acting as a straitjacket, preventing the baobab's growth and depriving it of food and moisture. **Above left and right:** The healthy dark green leaves of the figs are a sure sign that ultimately they will kill their baobab host.

THE AFRICAN BAOBAB

Looking at a baobab in the embrace of the thick, snaking trunk-roots of a fig, it is sometimes difficult to separate the strangler from the strangled. The outside of the wooden bole seems to be all fig, but inside, some of the baobab's trunk may still provide a conduit to channel nourishment to its branches. Often, the only way to gauge if the baobab is still a living, functioning organism is by examining the leaf canopy. When both fig and baobab are in leaf, fig leaves appear an even darker green. Although most African figs are deciduous, they may still be in leaf when baobabs are not; then the baobab branches protrude nakedly from the clusters of fig leaves, as if clutching vainly at the air for help.

Despite their name, strangler figs do not actually squeeze the life out of their host. The fig acts more like a straitjacket, enveloping the baobab trunk and preventing the host from growing. Slowly the fig begins to dominate the competition for water and light. The baobab trunk, no longer able to form any new sapwood, ages into heartwood and, after absorbing its own goodness, begins rotting away. Finally, the fig emerges as a perfect tree on its own.

Rain running down the branches deposits dust, dead leaves and nutrients in the fork of a baobab trunk. These micro-catchments stay damp much longer than the surrounding soil. As well as nourishing orchids and other epiphytes, they can prove such fertile growing grounds that almost any seed brought there by birds, small animals, wind or water stands a fair chance of germinating.

Apart from strangler figs, none of these accidental arrivals will cause the baobab much more direct harm than to add weight to already burdened branches. Of far more obvious danger are parasitic plants, which extract moisture and nourishment from their hosts. Some parasites, like mistletoe, have well-developed leaves with plenty of chlorophyll, and so can produce much of their own nourishment. Others have lesser or even no leaves and are more dependent on sustenance from the plants on which they are fixed.

The soil beneath deciduous trees is enriched by the humus of decomposing leaves. Both plants and fungi are attracted to this ideal growing ground, and some species have a particular affinity for the moist shade beneath baobab trees. African mushrooms usually have no English names, and the knowledge of their edibility and other ethnobotanical information often rests in the memories of a few tribal elders. Along the Kenya coast, the Giriama identify pink-gilled, slender-stalked mushrooms, growing only in the hollow trunks of fallen baobabs, as *zhoga muyu* – 'mushroom of the baobab'.

The taxonomy of African mushrooms has a long way to go; these ones, growing inside a fallen baobab trunk, may belong to the genus *Volvariella*.

In this parched landscape, elephants will gather whatever goodness they can from the baobab's trunk.

Surviving the mighty elephant

As well as the passive plant and fungal life living on or around baobabs, an array of birds and animals relies on the trees for necessities of life. Many of these smaller creatures spend their whole lives in the same tree, contributing to the composition of each baobab's own miniature ecosystem. Others visit for food, shelter and rest, or to raise their young. James Chapman, in *Travels in the Interior of South Africa* (1868), was struck by the baobab's great community:

Damage like this would kill any other species of tree, but this baobab showed a fine canopy of leaves.

> *'These trees are the resort of innumerable squirrels, mice, lizards, snakes, and also a small winged insect, called palele. When these insects alight on the human frame, they generally deposit a fluid, which soon induces a painful irritation and small white blisters. It seems to be a kind of vine-bug. Very fine hives, with honey, are often found in the baobab, and many of the larger birds delight to build their nests in them.'*

In his Appendix, Chapman details not only the uses to which local people put various parts of the tree, but also the shade and shelter it may give to 'troops of gnus, buffaloes and the mighty elephant himself'.

Baobabs are the biggest living things in their environments. Elephants are the largest land mammals on earth, and the longest-lived. They once wandered all over sub-Saharan Africa. Almost everywhere a baobab grew there were elephants, and the destinies of the two have been inextricably linked throughout their mutual evolution.

Today, although the extent of their coexistence is drastically reduced, baobabs and elephants still survive together. Elephants extract much goodness from baobabs, often at great cost to the trees, which are damaged to an extent that would easily kill any other species. To have survived so long in the African savanna, and yet to have continued appealing to elephants, baobabs needed unique resilience and powers of recovery. These they have, and elephant damage is seldom fatal.

Baobab bark is exceptionally rich in calcium, one of the reasons why elephants are so attracted to it. They first dig into the tree with their tusks, tearing the bark into strips and then ripping these off with their trunks. After that they may start on the wood, which is soft and moist, chewing it to extract nourishment before spitting out the stringy fibre.

Baobabs all over the plains and hillsides of Tanzania's Tarangire National Park show the full

THE AFRICAN BAOBAB

Elephants occasionally chew baobab twigs, but without any real enthusiasm for them; they prefer to dig away at the trunks.

spectrum of elephant damage. Scarcely a tree has gone untouched. Least affected are those whose bark was stripped off years ago, leaving scars far up the stem as the only evidence of elephants' attentions. Others have been lacerated more recently, and hanging off their trunks are tattered strips of grey and chestnut fibre, in contrast to the paler shreds of inner wood. Where elephants have lingered longer, great wedges have been gouged out of the trees.

The damage baobabs can seemingly sustain, while giving every indication of remaining in reasonable health, means revising some of the preconceived notions about what will kill a tree. The baobab's powers of survival are vastly superior to those of almost any other species. Some baobabs live with no more than half their trunk intact, appearing to defy the laws of both nature and gravity. As long as a baobab remains upright it seems to stay alive.

Elephants can work their way round younger baobabs until these are supported by no more than a thin central cylinder of wood, like the waist of an hourglass. Even if the tree does not fall over, a lot of moisture may be lost from its exposed trunk, leaving it more vulnerable to drought or disease. For older, hollow baobabs the mechanics of support and collapse are different. Having lost their heartwood centres, hollow trees depend on outer sapwood walls to keep them upright. If elephants gouge out too much from one side or the other, those trees will inevitably topple over.

If baobabs responded to damage as most other tree species do, they could never have endured so long in the face of elephant appetites. Baobabs needed to evolve an ability to withstand abnormally severe damage, and they have done. If they had not, to survive would have meant gradually developing other defences against elephants, like

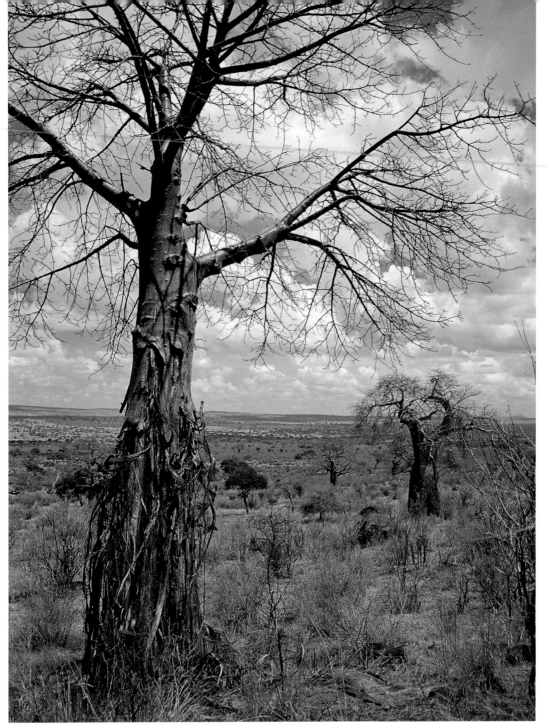

Elephants often target younger, more succulent, baobabs.

THE AFRICAN BAOBAB

ferocious thorns, a foul taste, much harder wood or poisonous sap. Yet for all the baobab's resilience, when the trees are truly stressed, elephants can damage whole populations so badly that these may look as if they will never recover. During a terrible drought in the early 1960s, elephants in Kenya's Tsavo National Park began to target baobabs so determinedly that they completely altered the park's landscape. Today, baobabs are far easier to find outside the park than in.

Even in that Utopian age, when elephants moved around Africa wherever they wished rather than wherever they could, populations of baobabs and elephants were likely to have continually fluctuated. The cycle of rain after drought after rain has sustained life in Africa since long before humans stood up. In wet times, many baobab seeds germinated and, with plenty of alternative food, the elephants allowed the trees to flourish. Then came dry years, which would be bad for both elephants and baobabs. Do these short-term imbalances not actually amount to long-term stability? And is the spur to evolutionary change not instability rather than equilibrium anyway?

In the context of their long lives, the elephants' range has contracted frighteningly fast, in two or three human generations, which is less than a single generation for baobabs. Just how fast is never better evidenced than by the elephant-scarred trunks of thousands of baobabs on what are now newly settled small-scale farms around the edges of national parks.

Living in harmony

Other creatures nourish themselves in decidedly less dramatic and less damaging ways on different parts of the tree. Flowers, fruit and leaves all provide sustenance for animals and birds with more delicate digestive systems than those of elephants. For some animals, at least one of these may be an important component of their diets; other animals may be merely tempted by morsels of flower or leaf in times of near-starvation.

Nectar is the pollinator's prime reward for visiting baobab flowers, but other creatures extract this thick sugary juice without contributing to the next generation of trees. Sunbirds manage to perch on the sepals and lean over to stick their beaks – perfectly curved for the operation – between the bases of petals, extracting nectar without going anywhere near the pollen-tipped stamens. Male scarlet-chested sunbirds look particularly magnificent in their search for sugar,

The baobab's fallen flowers seem to be one of nature's least utilized by-products, ignored by most creatures as a source of food, unlike seeds, which are avidly consumed by baboons before the pods are then invaded by insects.

their spectacular red chests, green heads and browny-black bodies in stark contrast to the creamy white flowers and brilliant blue of the sky. Green wood-hoopoes are shiny black, long-tailed birds with elegantly curved red beaks. They travel in noisy parties, always rushing to move on to the next tree. However, for a feast of baobab nectar they seem perfectly prepared to risk losing their companions, perching on nearby twigs and easily hooking their beaks between the sepals and petals of any flowers within reach.

With the countryside often so parched and barren when baobabs start blooming, their flowers may constitute food of last resort. In October some years ago, after six dry months, a few baobabs in Kenya's Meru National Park were showing early white blooms. One of these trees had been invaded by a troop of vervet monkeys, which seemed desperate to get at the flowers. These they first snapped off at the stalk before hurriedly pulling at the petals, which they dropped, together with the stamens, onto the ground. All that remained was stalk, sepals and the undeveloped ovary, but something there seemed to offer them a worthwhile bite. Sifting through the discards below the tree after the monkeys had left, and finding sepals and ovary still intact, I realized that what had probably attracted the monkeys were the globs of nectar they could lick from the underside of the sepals, after pulling off the rest of the flower. I have since heard of colobus monkeys behaving in the same way at the Kenya coast.

By daybreak, baobab flowers start to wilt, and when the corolla plops onto the ground, ants start searching for the sugary nectar. The petals wilt and darken, and the remains slowly crumble into dust. Tannin in the petals causes them to brown very quickly, and also makes them bitter tasting. There are very few written references to mammals -- usually impala or eland -- nibbling at freshly fallen flowers.

In this case though, the written record tells only part of the story. Munyao Mwakavi was a Wakamba driver, old enough to have some grey hairs and also to remember a much wilder environment than exists today. As a youth he would build a platform in a tree next to a flowering baobab, and wait with his bow and arrow for bushbuck to emerge in the evening from their daytime cover and start grazing on fallen flowers. Sometimes Munyao would even scatter handfuls of flowers below his perch, to give himself a better chance of shooting the animals cleanly. Now the bushbuck have gone, to be replaced by goats and sheep, and as soon as he let these out every morning, they too would scamper over to the nearest baobab to see if any flowers had fallen in the night.

Hungry animals are more attracted to the tender, pale green leaf shoots, which may also start appearing while the landscape awaits the first rains. If elephants are around, they will graze most of the twigs and greenery off the lower branches, leaving nothing within reach for any land-bound creature shorter than a giraffe. The best chance other herbivores get to feed on baobab leaves is offered by any newly fallen trees with roots still well enough connected to channel water up to the branches.

Cracks and hollows

Hollow baobab trunks make ideal bat roosts for many species of bizarre-sounding insectivorous bats – free-tailed, leaf-nosed, flat-headed and wrinkle-lipped to name just some. Fruit bats, particularly the Egyptian fruit bat, upon whose appetite the future of *Adansonia digitata* largely depends, usually roost by the thousand in caves. Quickly exhausting the local food supplies, they must often travel great distances to find fruit or flowers.

Late one afternoon, in coastal Tanzania, I had squeezed into a hollow baobab before my torch revealed the inner walls lined with twittering bats. Unsettled by the light, they began fluttering around, sensing they might be safer outside than in. The thought of these bats streaming past my face out of a hole I was partly blocking was enough to send me into reverse, until I noticed another chink of light further up the trunk. This was surely their exit and, with the torch beam off, calm soon returned. Easing

THE AFRICAN BAOBAB

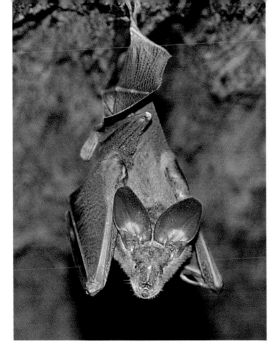

Its small eyes immediately identify this bat inside a hollow baobab as an echo-locating insectivore, perhaps one of the many species of free-tailed bats (Molossidae).

Harmless millipedes (Diplopoda) are particularly active at night and in the rainy season; they may find refuge in baobab trunks, but feed among leaf litter on the ground.

my way out, I waited until dusk to watch the bats leave their roost. As they spilled out of their baobab refuge, black against the grey sky over the grey sea, there seemed a satisfying symmetry in the thought that some of them might find baobab flowers to pollinate that night.

Cracks and wrinkles in the baobab bark, forks between branches, splintery stubs of broken limbs, rotting holes in the trunk – all provide wonderful shelters for insects and other small creatures. Geckos scuttle up and down the trunk in search of insects, flattening themselves against the bark. Out on the branch tips, weaving webs between the twig ends, are all sorts of spiders, including the buffalo spider, an arachnophobe's nightmare with big 'antlers' and black and red stripes on a bright yellow body.

One of the attractions of the baobab as a refuge, especially after many rainless months, is the water left in hollow trunks, or the moisture that remains in the soil around the roots. Reptiles need to drink, and arboreal snakes like the black mamba, boomslang

and twig snake may use baobabs as resting places until the rains come. Spitting or Egyptian cobras seek shelter in tree holes closer to the ground, and burrowing species of skinks will look for damp earth. Some agamas and other lizards are permanent members of a baobab's community; others move from tree to tree as the seasons prescribe.

Chameleons, which are also lizards, walk ponderously along shiny baobab branches, searching for insects to scoop up with their long, unfurling tongues. Green praying mantises live among the foliage, nabbing caterpillars off the leaves – that is if the females are not sated from devouring their mates. For most mantises, safety depends on being able to pose as twigs. Stick insects resemble mantises, although the two are not closely related. They too stalk around baobab branches, often at least one leg short of their full insect quota of six, in search of choice mouthfuls of vegetation, while avoiding the predatory attentions of ants, birds and lizards.

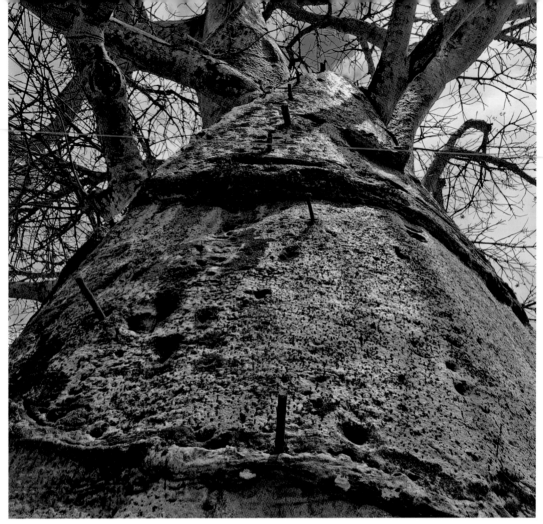

The pegs of a honey hunter's ladder are a sure sign that bees once nested in the tree, and may still do so.

Birds and bees

Honeybees also lodge in baobab trees, taking full advantage of clefts in the trunk or holes in branches to make their nests. Most of their food comes from other plants once these start flowering, although some bees may visit the flowers of their home tree in the early morning before blooms fall to the ground. Looking out for bees' nests on approaching a baobab is a wise precaution, and blundering up to a tree only to find bees buzzing in and out of a hole at eye level makes for a very nerve-wracking retreat.

Bees' nests can be difficult to spot, particularly in dry weather when their inhabitants are generally inactive. The waxy combs may be visible as they are darker than the baobab bark surrounding the nest hole. The hardwood sticks of human honey hunters' ladders, or footholds cut into the trunk, lead unerringly to nest sites, although the bees have often left these. Now, the only climbers may be baboons searching for fruit, or with the rising demand for baobab products, local people on a similar mission.

THE AFRICAN BAOBAB

The greater honeyguide, living up to its scientific name *Indicator indicator*, may lead humans to bees' nests in baobabs.

Baobab holes provide favoured nesting sites for yellow-billed hornbills. This male will feed his mate while she is walled inside her nest.

There is no more intriguing way to find a bees' nest than to be shown one by a greater honeyguide. At the southern end of the rocky backbone of Tarangire National Park is a huge hollow baobab, known, like many others elsewhere in Africa, as Poacher's Hideout. In April one year it was in full, luxuriant leaf, as was another nearby tree that offered shade for a midday picnic. Up above, a smallish, insignificantly plumaged bird began to fuss and flutter and, as soon as I reached for my binoculars, it flew down onto the top of a thorn bush. I made out distinctive pale cheeks, but was still struggling with identification when it took off again, this time into the leaves of the Poacher's Hideout. Convinced I had lost the bird among the foliage, I looked up and saw it fluttering away as if desperate I should keep it in sight. Then everything fell into place. Right next to the branch where it was displaying was a huge bees' nest, which the bird was showing me – playing the perfect role described for it by its scientific name *Indicator indicator*.

Many other birds perch, roost, nest and feed in baobabs. Most use the trees for no reason other than that they are the tallest and most hollow trees around. Parrots and their diminutives, lovebirds, have a close affinity with baobabs. Wherever their ranges overlap the birds seem greatly attracted

to the trees. They often nest in holes in the trunk, waddling clumsily around the branches, in distinct contrast to the screeching agility they show in the air, but in truth the trees provide very little of the shoots, fruit and small seeds that make up the diets of all species of *Poicephalus*.

Bigger baobab holes make good nest sites for several hornbills of the genus *Tockus*, particularly red-billed, yellow-billed, Von der Decken's and African grey. The females go to the dramatic lengths of sealing themselves into the holes with mud and droppings for the duration of incubation, as well as the first few weeks after the young have tapped their way out of their eggshells. During confinement the females lose all their feathers, while the monogamous males push fruit, insects and other small animals through the cracks left open in the earthen wall. Two or three weeks after the chicks have hatched, the female pecks open a hole large enough to squeeze through and then leaves the nest. The chicks reseal the hole, using their own droppings, leaving a slit into which both parents can now poke food. Seven weeks after hatching, the young ones finally exchange their keyhole view of the outside world for a panoramic sweep of African savanna.

Owls, barbets, woodpeckers and rollers roost or nest in baobab holes too. Owls also roost out in the

These marabou storks are using the baobab as no more than a lookout station.

open, often edging close up to the trunk in the hope of being less conspicuous and harder for small birds to mob. Rollers use the branches as lookout perches. I once watched a pair of lilac-breasted rollers courting outside a small hole in the trunk of a Tanzanian sea-edge baobab. The male fluttered excitedly around his mate, then they both launched into great sweeping circles of flight before he landed back on the lip of the hole and disappeared inside. The female waited quietly on the branch outside before the male emerged, and in that clumsy-seeming, yet extraordinarily elegant way of birds, fluttered on top of her and mated.

Perching is a serious business for rollers, which seem permanently on the watch for other birds entering their territories, as well as for food. Many raptors also use the tops of leafless baobabs as vantage points, especially those that hunt from perches. Brown snake eagles are especially associated with baobabs, often in cultivated areas where the trees have been spared. They too move from perch to perch, but need to spend much longer on each, searching for the slow slither of a hunting snake, often the cryptically camouflaged puff adder, which is favoured prey despite its size and toxicity. Wahlberg's eagles also watch over cleared ground between big trees. This small, almost kite-like predator regularly nests in baobabs. It never hunts birds near its home tree, and so weavers, starlings and other tree-dwellers are attracted to nest there by the protection from snakes that the eagle's presence offers.

Away from the trunk, other birds may be nesting, and down towards the end of the branches, where they are better protected from egg or nestling predators, weavers build their distinctive nests. Baobabs particularly suit those species that make nests of dry grass or twigs. Red-headed weavers construct untidy-looking nests with long entrance tubes; they are not communal nesters and if several nests are hanging off the end of the same slender branch it is usually because each year they build a new nest next to last season's. Near human habitation, baobabs are occasionally taken over

Red-billed buffalo weavers often build their untidy nests in baobab trees.

by noisy breeding colonies of black-headed weavers, seeking protection from predators by proximity to humankind.

The most conspicuous nests are the untidy communal structures built by red-billed buffalo weavers, which, from a distance, make baobabs seem afflicted by some parasitic growth. In true weaver fashion, only males build the nests, often over several months, before showing them to the females. They fortify their nests with acacia twigs as a further deterrent to invading snakes, like boomslangs, which inevitably try to reach the young birds. The following season, abandoned buffalo weaver nests may be taken over by superb starlings, which have higher comfort requirements than the former owners and line the nests with grass, but they still risk unwanted reptilian attentions.

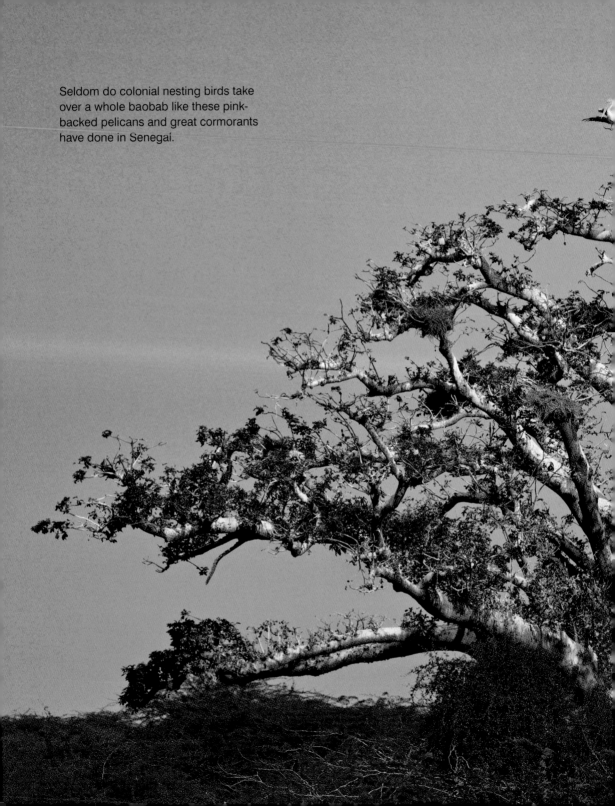

Seldom do colonial nesting birds take over a whole baobab like these pink-backed pelicans and great cormorants have done in Senegal.

In some places, buffalo weavers together with other weaver species are believed to nest only on the western side of a baobab, and so serve as a compass for disoriented travellers. In Namibia I looked at hundreds of buffalo weaver nests. There, the birds definitely seemed to favour the northern side of the trees, perhaps so the young could get as much sun as possible, while in Kenya, weavers appear to prefer the western branches. More likely though, weavers site their nests on the leeward side of a tree, where they are best protected from the wind. This would still allow nests to serve as direction finders, but only with the knowledge of the quarter from which the wind usually blows.

Take away the baobabs, and a whole community disappears with them. Shade, shelter, food, breeding places, hunting lookouts; the loss of a baobab is much more than the loss of a tree.

Still shattered by the after-effects of World War II, with the prospects of food rationing stretching on interminably, Britain's government conceived a massive scheme to alleviate the world's shortage of edible fats and oils: to cover more than three million acres of then-Tanganyika (now part of Tanzania) with peanuts. When lack of rain compounded the disasters afflicting the 'Tanganyika Groundnut Scheme', attempts were made to salvage something from its wreckage by planting sunflowers instead of peanuts. Early indications were that this might be successful, and in a letter to *The Times*, a Dr Harland calculated that to fill 24 000 acres would take 34 million sunflowers. Then another correspondent asked whether there were enough bees to pollinate all these sunflowers. As far as could be seen, there were almost no bees at all. Why were there no bees? Because after clearing the bush to prepare for the groundnut crops, scarcely any baobab was left for them to nest in!

These zebra and impala relish both the evening shade they get from the tree, and the grass that grows right up to its trunk.

THE AFRICAN BAOBAB

A FOREST IN ITSELF

CHAPTER SEVEN

A hermit in its shade

The baobab tree is some things to many people, and many things to some. It is food for humans and their animals, a pharmacy to treat tropical sickness, and a provider of raw materials for almost limitless uses. In the April 1962 issue of *Notes Africaines* from Senegal, J G Adam concludes that 'in reading of the variety of uses for the different parts of the baobab, a wise man would almost be tempted to take up the life of a hermit in its shade; he will lack for nothing in his life if he chooses his subject well'.

Like many birds, these Hadzabe hunters are getting a better view all round them from high up in a baobab tree.

A HERMIT IN ITS SHADE

Bark and fibre

The very essence of the baobab is contained in its trunk. The same regenerative powers that enable baobabs to survive excavations by elephants also allow bark to be harvested many times in the tree's life. The idea that a tree can easily survive repeated ringbarking takes some accepting and has astonished Europeans from David Livingstone onwards. In his *Missionary Travels* (1857), under the heading 'Vitality of the Mowana-Tree', he describes how:

'The natives make a strong cord from the fibres contained in the pounded bark. The whole of the trunk, as high as they can reach, is consequently often quite denuded of its covering, which in the case of almost any other tree would cause its death, but this has no effect on the mowana except to make it throw out a new bark, which is done in the way of granulation. This stripping of the bark is repeated frequently, so that it is common to see the lower five or six feet an inch or two less in diameter than the parts above.'

Beneath the grey layer of outer bark, past the green chlorophyll, is the inner, paler fibre, which has more uses than a ball of string. This is removed in strips and moistened (sometimes by chewing), then pounded, before being twisted together into cords of varying thickness. Robust individuals of several tree species can occasionally survive ringbarking, but the ability of *Adansonia digitata* to tolerate the repeated removal of wide encircling panels makes it unique in Africa.

The first Europeans to witness the debarking of baobabs could not believe the trees could possibly survive, as this one in Benin clearly has.

The Kenyan National Archives has a fascinating exchange of correspondence concerning the use of baobab parts. It begins in 1917 with the Conservator of Forests writing to the Colony's Acting Chief Secretary, suggesting rules be promulgated for the protection of baobabs on Crown land. The letter is copied to the Provincial Commissioner in Mombasa, who adds: 'I now observe that natives are also removing the bark from these trees and would ask that any such Rule should contain provision for the preventing of such removal'. Back and forth go official missives between coast and capital until reason ultimately prevails and the suggestion is turned down, influenced perhaps by the Commissioner of Police noting that '… it would be only fair if the headmen were told to tell all their

THE AFRICAN BAOBAB

Above: Bark is usually harvested from the trunk, but, for bow strings, this Hadzabe hunter in Tanzania preferred to strip it from young branches at the top of the tree.
Right: Bark from bigger trees is often stripped off in panels. The marks on this baobab near Mwingi in Kenya show it to have a long history of providing bark for the local community.

villagers before any action is taken; the custom of cutting bark is of long standing'.

The inhabitants of coastal Kenya were apparently twisting short lengths of cord to bundle up firewood and personal belongings. Elsewhere, thin strips of woven bark were making fishing lines, nets and strings for bows or musical instruments. In his 1863 *Journal of the Discovery of the Source of the Nile*, Captain James Grant refers to 'rope and kilts' being made from baobab bark.

Almost everywhere baobabs grow, their bark is stripped and plaited. The twisted fibres of baobab bark harness donkeys, mules or oxen to their carts, while thicker bundles make ropes with which the Dogon people in Mali haul their dead into burial caves on the cliff side. The cord itself can be woven into mats, and if the weave is tight enough the fibre may be used to make cups and other containers

All over Africa, women roll lengths of baobab fibre along their thighs, then plait them together into long lengths of cord.

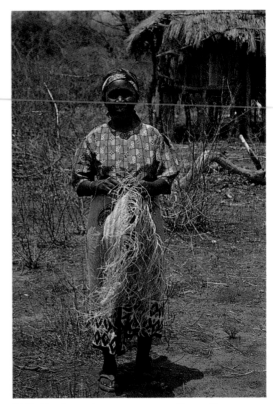

Skilled basket makers can weave as they walk.

for liquid. Cord can also be turned into coarse cloth, waterproof hats in Senegal, fabric for shoes in Zanzibar, or fibre filters for sieving traditional honey brew elsewhere in Tanzania.

The Wakamba in Kenya hoist up beehives and lower down containers of honey with baobab bark ropes, and also make particularly fine baskets called *kiondos*. They prefer to harvest fibres from young trees, small enough to be encircled with the arms of a single adult. Fibres are usually stripped off in metre lengths, and are separated from the outer bark by pounding them with the same large pestle that crushes grain.

Some years ago I met Rosemary Syungo Mwenbakau, the chair of the Mitamisyi Location basket-making group in central Kenya's Mwingi District. The group was weaving baskets from baobab yarn and selling them through marketing centres established by various aid organizations. To make the yarn, Syungo had her children chew the strips of fibre to moisten them; once these were soft and pliable she would roll one length with another on her thigh, and in that way make up long, easily portable, skeins.

Natural fibres vary in colour from dark brown, through pink to straw. Syungo showed me how fibres could be blackened by rubbing them in soot on the bottom of a clay cooking pot. Deep dark red colour was once obtained from stones in the distant Tana River; but weavers were finding it easier to extract the pigment by boiling up roots and dark-coloured chips of wood.

With the arrival of Europeans in Africa, human impact on many natural resources shifted from traditional, sustainable harvest to mechanized over-exploitation. Trees that had once provided local communities with food, shelter or medicine were suddenly in demand for use in a previously inconceivable range of goods for Western markets. It was fortunate for the baobab that its bark could be harvested without long-term damage to the trees, because the fibre proved a popular ingredient in a particularly eclectic list of products. The 1908

This basket was made by Rosemary Syungo Mwenbakau using baobab yarn. Some of the colours are natural; others are obtained from soot and dyes.

Bulletin of Miscellaneous Information from the Royal Botanic Gardens at Kew reported baobab being used in Angola for 'sacking and wrappers . . . for the conveyance of cotton, gum, copal, and orchella weed'; in India for elephant saddles; and elsewhere for helmets, caps and ladies' hats. Before the advent of the breech-loading rifle, plugs of baobab wood were apparently also in use as wadding in muzzle-loading rifles.

If the traditional harvest of bark never posed a threat to the health of local baobab populations, the same certainly could not be said for the appetite of the paper industry, particularly in South Africa. Pulp came from the wood of the baobab, rather than its bark, and this of course meant cutting down the tree. The paper was used to print currency for India, and also served as rough packaging in England. Only the difficulties of bleaching and water extraction saved the tree trunks from ending up in a far wider range of paper products and it took a public outcry from both within and without South Africa to force the legislation, which in 1941 finally protected baobabs from that country's paper mills.

High moisture content has spared baobabs from far more than being pressed into paper. Above all, it makes the wood all but useless as firewood, charcoal or building material, and it is no surprise that in West Africa the Hausa word for it is *fanko* – in this context translated as 'good for nothing'. When a baobab finally collapses and starts to crumble, the rotting fibres make an excellent fertilizer to spread back on the land from which the tree emerged, but such benefit is certainly not enough to justify the effort of actually felling a tree.

A hollow trunk

Besides the bark, the greatest attribute of a large baobab tree trunk is its emptiness. In the daily grind of rural life, the opportunity to use empty baobab trunks as stores or shelters is far too valuable to ignore. Whatever the availability of branches, skins, dung or earth, constructing shelter in Africa consumes time, energy, resources and sometimes money. Baobabs are often hollow by a relatively early age, and the ready-to-inhabit, waterproof refuges they provide seldom pass unappreciated. If nature or elephants have not created an entrance to the hollow trunk, this is easily made with the help of a hand axe. The eventual uses to which these natural havens are put ultimately depends on the immediate needs of the community, influenced perhaps by prevailing systems of tribal land ownership.

Ibn Battuta was inspired as much by the hollowness of the baobabs he saw in the Kingdom of Mali in 1353 as by their size, passing one where there was '... a man inside weaving; he had set up his loom and was weaving. I was amazed at him.' More often, hollow baobabs make homes, shops and storage space for everything from road-mending tools and bicycles to animal feed. Some

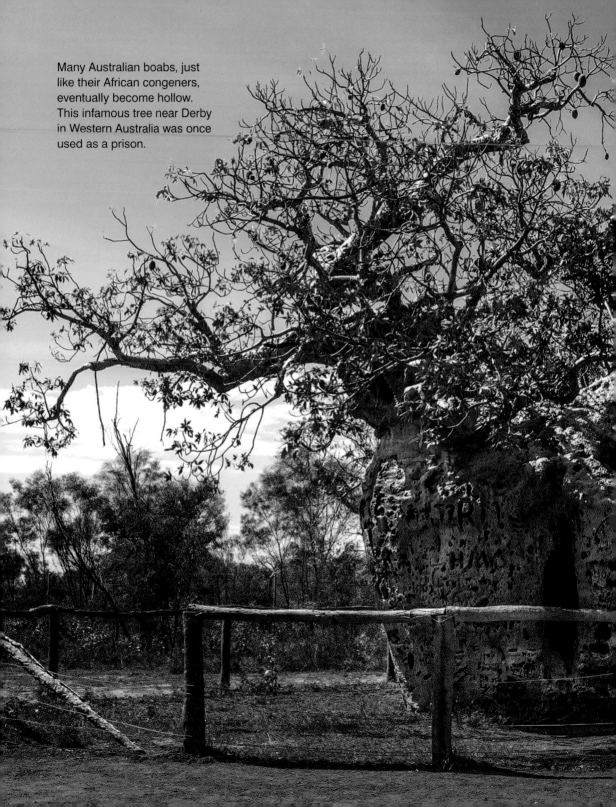

Many Australian boabs, just like their African congeners, eventually become hollow. This infamous tree near Derby in Western Australia was once used as a prison.

hollow baobabs have doubled as stables, meeting places and a dairy, and trees growing beside well-travelled roads are likely to serve as bus shelters. A baobab at Duiwelskloof was once fitted out as a watering hole for human visitors, and another South African tree served as a beer store for a nearby bar.

Local administrations in remote areas without prisons have sometimes incarcerated offenders in baobab trunks, both in Australia and Africa. Immediately outside the police station in Kasane, in northeastern Botswana, stands an ancient baobab. Partially collapsed, in 2004 the tree was proudly floodlit, notwithstanding or possibly even because of its history as the women's prison. My guide seemed embarrassed by this history, but somehow reassured by the presence of a basket in the entrance, in which dozed a yellow and black lizard next to a folded square of paper. With Botswana then having the highest AIDS infection rate in the world, had one of its sufferers scrawled a cry for help on this missive? The prison tree still stands and visitors can freely enter its cavity to imagine themselves in gaol.

Further north, in Katima Mulilo, on the banks of the Zambezi, grows one of the most renowned baobabs on the African continent, converted with some ingenuity, but wanton disrespect, into a flush lavatory. The tree is on a road junction in the old administrative centre, next door to the local SWAPO office, from which loud Lingala music was blasting when I called by. The baobab's expanding roots had wedged the door immovably ajar, allowing anyone to see inside, but not enter. Some time later, the door was removed and now the curious are kept at a distance by a wire fence around the tree.

Elsewhere, in what is now northern Botswana, baobabs have served as informal postboxes. Hunters, prospectors, missionaries and others living on the edge of the Kalahari wastes would leave their correspondence in the tree, for passers-by heading for South Africa to post there. Likewise, anyone travelling north would pick up mail for those same lonely migrants, and drop it in the baobab poste restante for collection.

Salaita Hill, near Taveta in southern Kenya, was the scene of one of many actions fought by the elusive German general, Paul von Lettow-Vorbeck, to tie down vastly superior numbers of Allied troops during World War I. The hill guarded the strategically important Taveta Gap through the line of mountains running east from Kilimanjaro. In the dry February heat of 1916, South African soldiers were struggling to dislodge the Germans from their entrenched positions on the slopes. Grossly underestimating the strength of their enemy, the South Africans were ultimately forced to retreat, and to compound their casualties, a hidden sniper kept picking off soldiers from the rear. This much is fact, but at least some of what comes next may be the product of an urge not to let the truth get in the way of a good story.

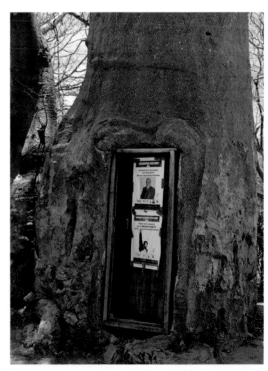

The famous tree in Katima Mulilo, which was converted into a flush lavatory; with the door wedged shut its only practical use in 2004 was to advertise the forthcoming Namibian elections.

This baobab near Salaita Hill in Kenya is said to have provided the hideout for a German sniper during World War I.

Eventually, the German general withdrew, almost vaporizing, as he so often did, and nowhere have I been able to find the identity of this Valkyrie, nor whose soul she would sweep off to Valhalla.

Not only the living, but also the dead found shelter in baobabs, and in Senegal hollow trunks were the final resting places for the bodies of some of the Serer people. Alive, griots were semi-outcasts, which, as they were musicians, clowns, fortune-tellers, general entertainers, gurus and professional praise-singers to the famous, seems particularly unfair. Somehow, their fellow human beings seemed unable to accept and absorb them into normal life – or normal death. For griots, the final resting place was a hollow baobab, their enshrouded bodies suspended inside the trunk by their followers, who feared that if they were buried underground, their knowledge would die with them. Otherwise their remains were piled up in heaps in empty trees,

Attached to the Allied troops were local Wakamba askaris who, for reasons long forgotten, had been banned from taking snuff. They knew the sniper's hideout, or so the story goes, but refused to reveal it so long as the ban continued. Reluctantly, the South African officers relented, whereupon the askaris lifted their arms together and all pointed to a distant baobab. When the soldiers finally surrounded the sniper's refuge, they found a woman inside.

The tree is easy to find, and has a gaping hole in the top of the trunk where the branches fork. I jumped down into the hollow to look for bullet cases, and to imagine this unlikely fighter crouched there for days on end, victualled they say by faithful Taveta retainers. The story has many different endings – that she was blasted by shell-fire, shot resisting capture, or taken prisoner. Variations on these themes add a father into the tree; others more romantically suggest she was avenging the death of a German lover.

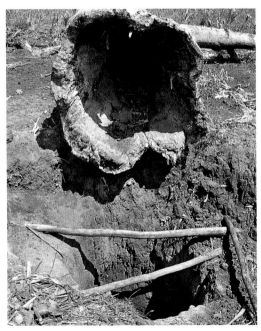

Many wells make use of the hollow trunk of the baobab, but here the cavity left by the rotted root has created water storage capacity.

slowly mummifying. These peculiar burial rites may survive in remote areas, but mostly live on only in anthropological papers, the memories of tribal elders and the memoirs of French colonial administrators.

In no way is the living human body better nurtured by hollow baobabs than when they fill up with water. It seems strange that the use of these cavities as wells is not nearly as widespread as the trees are. Obviously usage is fuelled by necessity and in those blessed pockets of baobab-strewn Africa with no serious shortage of water, its storage is of little concern. But where most baobabs grow, water is scarce, and maintaining a supply throughout the dry times may literally be a matter of life and death. In the absence of cement, corrugated iron or a good hole in the ground, baobabs make extremely effective wells, and if nature does not hollow them out, humans are perfectly able to do so.

The best-known baobab wells are probably still those in Kordofan in central Sudan, where baobabs were known by the Berber name *tebeldi*. If old age had not hollowed out the trees naturally, Hamar tribes would excavate the centres with axes and

knives, causing no more apparent injury to the baobab's wellbeing than human bark strippers or stressed elephants. The process is well described in the *Geographical Journal* (1910) by Captain Watkiss Lloyd, one-time governor of Kordofan:

> 'The baobab trees have to be carefully prepared for use as reservoirs. The large branches are first cut off near the trunk. If this is not done, the trunk is apt to split as soon as it is hollowed out.
>
> A hole is cut in the trunk, generally just above a branch, which serves as a platform for the man who is filling the tree, and the interior is hollowed out. Round the bottom of the tree a shallow basin some 20 or 30 feet in diameter is made, in which the rain-water collects. As soon as there is a storm, the people go out and fill their trees.
>
> The water so stored remains perfectly good until the end of the next hot weather, or even longer. A few trees, naturally hollow, have a hole at the top between the branches, and fill themselves, the branches catching the water and acting as gutters. These are called lagai and are highly valued by the Hamars.'

A caravan finds shelter beneath a shady baobab in Cape Verde. This illustration was published in an 1861 edition of *Le Tour du Monde*, a French travel journal.

THE AFRICAN BAOBAB

These *tebeldis* may still play a crucial role in Sudanese society. Nowhere are there likely to have been enough natural baobab wells to sustain permanent settlement, and until people began hollowing out the trees artificially, most of Kordofan would only have supported nomads. It is not an exaggeration to say that many villages exist only because nearby baobabs store water through the dry months. Long-term settlements quickly degrade marginal land, and the wells quite possibly end up watering more people than the land itself is capable of supporting.

Tebeldis had enormous value in areas where the notion of private landownership prevails, and can be sold, argued about, fought over or handed down from one generation to the next like ancestral heirlooms. Many are prefaced with *Um*, Arabic for mother, followed by a word connected with water or some other marked characteristic of the particular tree. *Um Dhirifa* means 'the tearful', which may allude to the tree's leaking, *Um Laqui* (anglicized to 'lagai' by Lloyd) are the wells that fill naturally, while *Um Asal* (honey) describes a tree in which bees are nesting.

While the dependence on baobab wells in Kordofan is almost unique, the tree's natural capacity to store water has certainly not been lost on the inhabitants of other parts of Africa. Ibn Battuta remarked on baobabs in 14th-century Mali that collected drinkable water, and the San in Namibia and Botswana still rely on baobab cisterns to help them travel through the otherwise waterless wastes of the Kalahari. The San suck the water from the bottom of tree cisterns through long straws made out of interconnected reeds – 'sipping sticks'.

Bees in trees

Hollows in branches are often taken over by bees, and all over Africa, wooden pegs hammered into baobab trunks lead up to their nests. The pegs are made of ebony, *Combretum* or other hard wood, and often outlast the tenure of the bees. These prongs linger on, as much part of the tree's history as the elephant scars on its bark. If bees

Hadzabe honey hunters near Lake Eyasi in Tanzania hammer successive hardwood pegs into the trunk of a baobab to help them climb the tree.

Bees are encouraged to inhabit artificial hanging
hives if there are not enough natural nesting
places for them. Honey is usually harvested at
night, hives first being lowered to the ground
and the bees stupefied by smoke.

Hanging bee hives on smooth-barked trees like baobabs helps spare them from the attentions of honey badgers.

lust for honey is so strong that they will attack dogs and even humans in their way. Once up the tree, honey badgers raid any hives within reach, and access others by gnawing off supporting branches or ropes, then breaking open the fallen hives on the ground.

A hundred other uses

Supporting the baobab's massive bulk is a shallow network of roots. The bark on the bigger roots can be twisted into ropes, much as can that on the trunk, and the hole left by the roots of a fallen tree sometimes makes a water store. There seems to be enough nutrition – and an almond-like taste – in the thinner, terminal roots for these to be worth simmering and chewing in times of real food shortages. Seedling roots are much more tender and their seasonal scarcity makes them something of a delicacy, particularly the swollen, radish-like taproot.

Leaves, flowers and fruit on the tree nourish different birds and animals. Herbivores graze the leaves if they can reach them, antelopes and livestock nibble fallen petals, and baboons crack open the pods and swallow the contents. Birds probe around the flowers for nectar, insects invade the fallen fruit, and smaller mammals scurry off into the undergrowth with seeds. Small wonder, therefore, that omnivorous humans also find baobab produce the source of much goodness.

The knowledge that parts of certain plants are palatable may be inherited or learnt, or perhaps even acquired in more ethereal ways. To keep knowledge alive it needs to be used, and fundamental to knowing how to use any particular plant is its presence. Yet even where baobabs grow, this goodness often goes unappreciated.

Most of those living around baobab trees know that the leaves make good eating. 'Good' is relative, and in the more fertile parts of baobab country local inhabitants seldom resort to eating baobab leaves or feeding them to livestock, and the trees retain the full-branched look, quite unlike those in Eritrea

need further encouragement, or more appealing nest sites, artificial hives are suspended from the baobab's great spreading branches, sometimes hanging all over the tree like a crop of giant oblong fruit.

The most enthusiastic beekeepers in Kenya are the Wakamba, much of whose homeland is populated with baobabs. They hollow out *Commiphora* branches to make hives, closing them with lids at either end and chipping out a small entrance hole in the bottom. To attract bees, hives are smeared inside with beeswax and aromatic leaves before being hoisted up into the branches. Having adopted a hive, the bees then begin breeding, successive generations sometimes occupying the same one for 15 years or more.

Bees nesting naturally in baobabs do so because of the hole, not because the tree offers any particular biological or chemical attraction. Apart from the baobabs' size and their magnificent spreading branches, which are ideal for hanging hives from, the Wakamba also like the trees for their smooth bark, which makes them difficult for honey badgers to climb. These powerful creatures, also known as ratels, are completely fearless, and their

THE AFRICAN BAOBAB

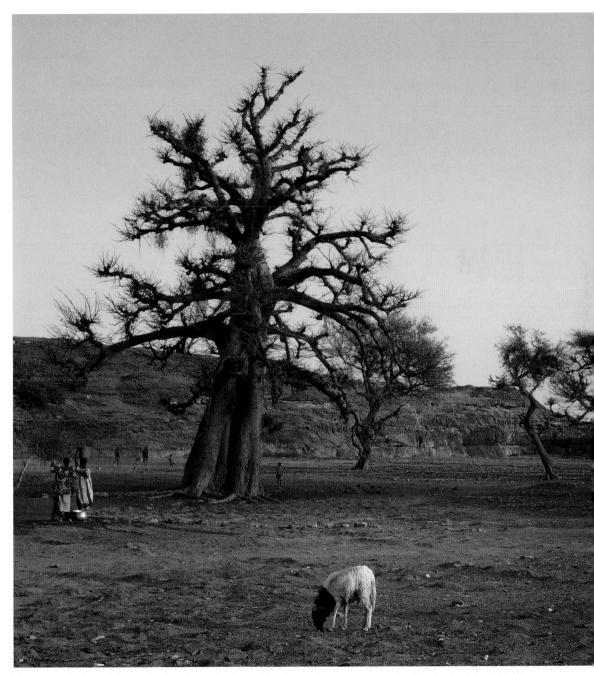

The leaves of this west African baobab have clearly provided the local community with food for livestock and maybe even for humans too.

This Eritrean baobab has been drastically cut back in the course of harvesting its leaves, and fewer branches will mean fewer flowers and so less fruit.

through the year, they must be dried then stored, either in powdered form or whole. Leaves dry quickly and easily in the sun, but this destroys their carotene, which is a source of vitamin A. Much better is to dry them slowly in the shade. In the language of the Wolof people of Senegal, powdered leaves are known as *lalo*, and there, as elsewhere, they are used to season and thicken stews, make sauces and add to couscous or local porridge. Like pulp and oil, the dried leaves are now finding a ready commercial market far beyond where the trees grow. *Poudre de feuilles de lalo* or *poudre de feuilles de baobab* are now freely advertised on the internet as tonics for hair and skin.

When even dried food is running out, fresh baobab blooms will not be ignored, if not as a source of food, then at the very least as a flavour for drink. The pollen can be mixed with water to make a reasonable glue, and an erstwhile owner of the Baobab Café (now Lukmaan's Restaurant) in the Old Town of Zanzibar remembers creating dolls out of baobab flowers, with petals making up the skirts

or the Sahel. There, the annual harvest of greenery stunts baobab limbs, and is bought at the price of far fewer fruit from these pollarded trees.

Leaves are at their tastiest and most nutritious when they are pale greeny-yellow, tender, soft and small. They can then be eaten straight or boiled up and added to soup. My first efforts at cooking baobab foliage met with little success as I watched my guests shovelling in forkfuls of greenery before awkwardly removing long stringy fibres from their mouths. Only after I learnt to pull the two halves of the leaf off their coarse central ribs before cooking was this spinach-like delicacy truly appreciated.

Fresh leaves adorn market stalls for very few months, and to make the supply of leaves last

Humans have carefully cleaned out all the seeds from these pods.

THE AFRICAN BAOBAB

and stamens the hair. Sometimes she would spend hours plucking pollen from the stamens, and end by whispering to her flower-doll, 'Pretty baby, your hair is now clean'.

If bats or bushbabies have done their work, small fruit will start appearing on the ends of the baobab branches where the flowers once were, slowly enlarging over the coming months. By the time the seeds are ripe, embedded in their white acidic pulp, the tree is usually leafless, dripping with the baubles of hard-shelled pods.

The pulp's most notorious component is its vitamin C (ascorbic acid). Different analyses report it to be anything between four and ten times richer in vitamin C than are oranges. All agree it is the richest known natural source of the vitamin, which promotes healing and is particularly important for healthy bones and tendons. The pulp also contains tartaric acid, sometimes called cream of tartar. When added to baking powder this makes an essential ingredient in baking bread and baobab fruit pulp has often been used as a substitute for cream of tartar, not least in the field kitchens of both British and German armies during World War I. Not for nothing was the tree once known in South Africa as *kremetartboom* ('cream of tartar tree')!

The baobab pulp's vitamin C content is probably the most important reason for the tree's dispersal round the Indian Ocean coast, as well as over to the West Indies. On long sea journeys, fruit pulp would have provided a perfect source of vitamin C, easily stored, long-lasting, and a powerful antidote to scurvy that was long ignored by the British navy.

Scurvy is a result of vitamin C deficiency and takes around six months to manifest itself. George Anson's round-the-world voyage was just one of many badly afflicted by the disease. Starting out from England in 1740 at the head of six vessels and 2 000 men, Anson returned four years later with a mere 200 men in a single ship. At that point he was losing up to ten sailors a day from a condition whose symptoms were described by his chaplain, Richard Walter, as including:

'… large discoloured spots over the whole surface of the body, swelled legs, putrid gums … extraordinary lassitude of the whole body … ulcers of the worst kind attended with rotten bones, and such a luxuriancy of fungous flesh as yielded to no remedy.'

Stocking up at one of the West African ports with baobab fruit would have saved hundreds of lives. Captain James Cook suspected that fresh vegetables kept the disease at bay during the first of his three epic voyages, in 1768, but not until 1795 were British naval ships issued with lime juice, giving rise to the generally derogatory epithet 'limey' used to describe a British person.

Repeatedly knocking pods before breaking them open helps separate pulp from seeds, otherwise this is best done by adding the pod's contents to water and stirring the mixture with

Royal Naval surgeon James Lind was one of the first doctors to appreciate that citrus fruit cured scurvy.

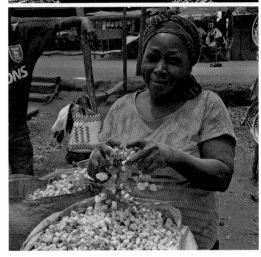

Top: Sucking these sweets and spitting out the pips may help disperse the seeds. **Middle:** In eastern Kenya pith and seeds are separated by first soaking the contents of the pod in water, then agitating the mixture with a special stirring stick. **Above:** With the increased commercial demand for baobab seeds, these are now collected up by the sackful.

a forked stick. When mixed with water or milk (which it curdles), pulp produces a healthy and refreshing drink, somewhat acid tasting, rather like sherbet. This can be sweetened by adding sugar or honey, and the mixture can be condensed into quite an acceptable jam. Along the East African coast the pulp is flavoured with coconut, and the mixture thickened into a sauce for enlivening maize meal, ground guinea corn or other local versions of porridge.

Where power supplies are consistent enough to keep water iced, baobab pulp, water and sugar, together with cloves or nutmeg, are frozen into a delicious sorbet-style confection. Children crowd round Malian bus stops, with cool boxes around their necks loaded with lollipops – red ones flavoured with hibiscus flowers and milky-white ones with the pulp of the baobab fruit. Seeds coated in coloured sugar are sold in packets all along the East African coast. The spat-out pips littering the pavements in Zanzibar's Stone Town are giveaway signs of a *madrasa* (Koranic school) behind an ornately carved door.

Pulp smoulders slowly enough to make a good insect repellent, or to smoke fish and, perhaps inevitably, also finds its way into traditional alcohol. The Wasandawe of central Tanzania are just one of many African tribes who make a brew of baobab pulp, adding water, flour and yeast.

Both local and international demand for baobab powder has exploded over the past decade, as its benefits have been better analyzed and appreciated by ever more health-conscious consumers. Halfway between Nairobi and Mombasa is a small town called Mtito Andei. While exploring a nearby village, I met Stella, who was presiding over at least three enormous sacks of pulp-covered baobab seeds. These, she told me, were to be collected for transport to Mombasa, although she had very little idea what would happen to them down there. No matter, collecting them from nearby trees will have given good pocket-money to many local folks, and long may the demand continue.

THE AFRICAN BAOBAB

The seeds are also nutritious, rich in protein and potassium. However, to become remotely palatable they either need cooking, fermenting, or at least pounding up. Roasting makes seeds brittle and easier to grind, either to use like coffee in hot drinks or to make a culinary flavouring. If the outer husks can be removed, the kernels provide an excellent edible oil, full of fat, as well as calcium, thiamine and iron, with even more vitamin B1 than ground nuts or rice bran. Katong balls are a Ghanaian food, made by pounding fried seeds and water into a paste, which is then fermented for two days before rolling into balls ready for frying or adding to soup.

Baobab oil seems to have much wider external than internal uses. Mashed seeds have been used for centuries to make shampoos for Swahili women. Now, as is so often the case, commercial use is starting to mirror long-standing tradition, and many companies are seeking to promote the cosmetic benefits of the oil especially as a tonic for skin and hair. And even the red fibres to which the seeds are connected (funicles) are now finding markets, including as a raw material for paper-making or in an antioxidant tea.

Enclosing the pulp and seeds is the velvety pod – a multi-shaped, all-purpose container. Old pods, still full of seeds, can make fishing floats or be rattled to the beat of traditional music. Once emptied of their natural contents, the only restrictions on their uses are the limits of human imagination. This has produced flower pots, water containers, snuff boxes, drums, carved decorations, lamp and candle shades, canoe paddles and a host of other utilitarian articles. Pods burn well, and the resulting ash, rich in potassium, makes fertilizer and soap. And if there is anything left over after all that, powdered pods are even said to be worth smoking or adding to snuff.

Necessity is the mother of invention, and it surely drove the discovery of many of the benefits conferred on local communities by the baobab tree. Yet the impetus to such a discovery is obviously muted by the availability of alternatives. If vines grew

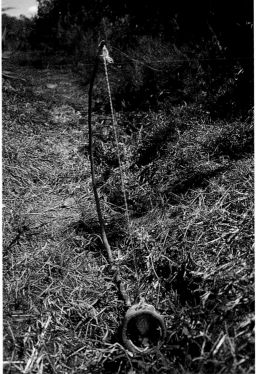

Top: Empty baobab pods make good rat traps on the East African coast; maize kernels lure the rodent into the trap, and nibbling at the food triggers a noose that tightens around its neck. **Above:** The curved stick forms the spring-loading mechanism that tightens the noose.

all over baobab trees, offering long, strong stems as ready-made ropes, the potential of baobab fibre for the same purpose might still be locked up in the tree trunk. In wetter parts of the baobab's range, blessed with a greater diversity of plant life, there are more potential sources of food for humans or livestock than where the baobab protrudes almost alone out of scrubby semi-desert.

On much of the East African coast, average annual rainfall is well over 100 cm, and residents are favoured with an abundant supply of alternative sources of food. Some of them eat baobab leaves and fruit pulp, but generally the only serious activity around the baobab is scraping out pulp-covered seeds to sugar-coat and sell as confectionery, and more recently to service the demand for the pulp itself to process into powder.

In Zanzibar it is even harder to find anyone who does anything with any part of the baobab except to make bonbons (*mabuyu*). No one even seems to mix pulp into sauces or vitamin drinks. Nearly every leaf on every Zanzibari baobab sees out its full four- or five-month natural span, immune from harvest for either human or animal consumption. Compared to the harshest parts of the baobab's range, like the Sahel or the northern Kalahari, most of Zanzibar is a proverbial land of milk and honey. The sea and its bounty are never far away, rain falls regularly, and at any time of year huge arrays of fruit and vegetables are displayed on roadside stalls. This super-abundance of local produce seems to have rendered the baobab's products superfluous. Was it always so? Until the arrival of all this extra sustenance, the baobab must surely have provided the inhabitants of Zanzibar with more than pips to suck and the odd pair of bark-rope sandals?

Shade from the midday African sun is one of the greatest benefits any big tree can grant to human or animal.

THE AFRICAN BAOBAB

A HERMIT IN ITS SHADE

CHAPTER EIGHT

The healing tree

Wherever baobabs grow, they are central to traditional healing practices. Medicinal compounds are extracted from fruit, wood and leaves. The trees and the ground around them serve as stages for rituals of treatment. Baobabs are vital in sustaining local people, both culturally and nutritionally. So utterly do they dominate their landscapes, and so long do they endure, it takes no great leap of belief to revere them as homes of spirits or at least conduits to the ethereal world beyond. Animists still imbue the tree with its own spirit. Other Africans, whose spiritual lives also remain uncluttered by the strictures of modern religion, find the base of a huge baobab somewhere to pray to a god that may be everywhere, but is surely more there than anywhere else.

The young leaves on this tree promise to provide shade, food, medicine and so much more.

THE AFRICAN BAOBAB

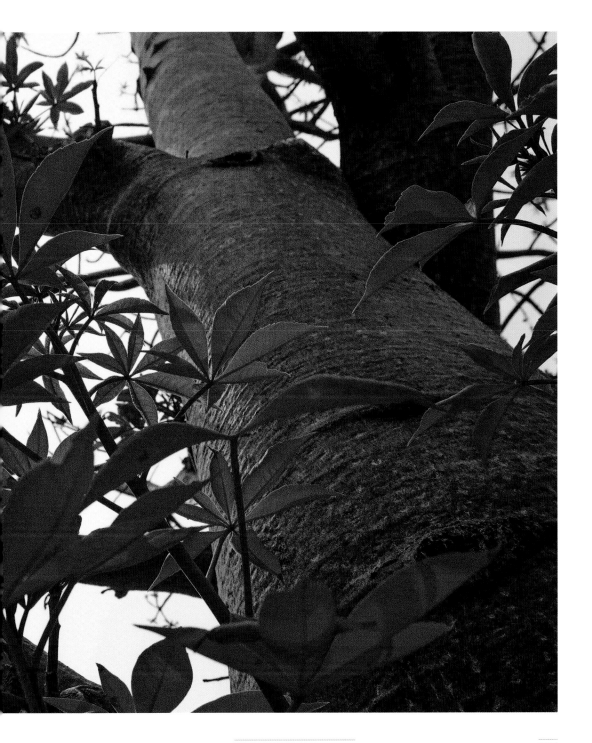

A tree of hope

Kenyatta Drive runs along the more developed length of the seafront in Dar es Salaam. In the garden of Number 12, where Roald Dahl once lived, was a gigantic baobab, so huge that the plot's perimeter wall curved to accommodate the trunk. On the other side of the road is a much smaller baobab on a piece of open grassland, above low coral cliffs dropping down to the beach. The smaller tree was once studded with thousands of dhow nails, each of which fixed a prayer or talisman to the trunk.

These pleas were written on folded squares of paper and, when I was there some years ago, the more recent ones had still not disintegrated in the tropical monsoon storms. Some of the nails impaled objects used in the course of tree-side ceremonies. From a branch hung a black bag, spiked with protruding porcupine quills, the dried skin of a pufferfish swung in the wind, and ragged bits of cloth fluttered from twigs and trunk like Buddhist prayer flags.

So many dreams, prayers, great hopes and much disappointment were all bound up in the hapless baobab. The tree itself seemed to suffer neither from the burden of so much collective expectation, nor from serving as a giant pincushion. It was not yet large enough to generate the particular reverence accorded huge and ancient trees, and no one I spoke to referred to this baobab's supernatural attributes. Rather, it was a tree that was then accessible to all, and so provided a platform for rituals of healing and help.

One sticky afternoon, the tree's magnetic promise drew two Swahili women to its shelter. I assumed them to be mother and daughter, shepherded by a man who was clearly a traditional healer. The girl sat down, her legs out towards the trunk, while the other two fussed around her. The man began applying a floury white powder to the girl's face, and the mother then passed her hands seven times around her daughter's head. After more ceremony and loud incantations, the healer took

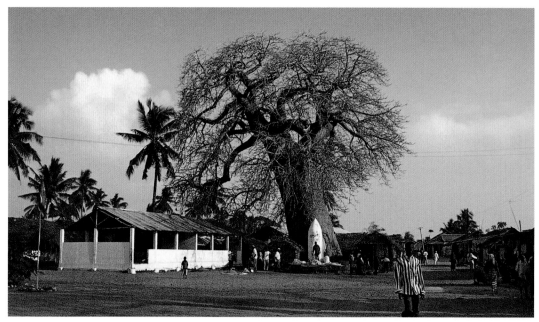

Religion and animism seem to meet in this shrine of tree and coral rock in Mocímboa da Praia in northern Mozambique.

THE AFRICAN BAOBAB

The trunk of the former healing tree in Dar es Salaam, into which thousands of dhow nails had been hammered, some of which affixed prayers and others pieces of clothing or fetishes.

a thin strip of bark from the tree and tied it to the girl's hair – an amulet to protect against continued infertility? Shortly after they had left, a ragged youth bore his troubles to the tree, alone. He left an offering to his god – broken coconut, bottles of dark red liquid, and a bright red cloak. The act of breaking the coconut may have been symbolic of the release of evil from his system.

Since that day I have returned twice to that tree. On the first occasion, I took a taxi from the airport and asked the driver to park nearby while I wandered and watched. He refused to wait for me near the tree, perhaps sensing that there were many disturbed spirits around, cast out during healing rituals and searching for new corporeal resting places. Even if it meant losing a fare, this was one

risk he was not prepared to take. My second return visit was a huge disappointment, although much less to me than it must have been to all those who had pinned so much hope on the tree. Having completed a day of mediation training nearby, I took my fellow tutors down to visit the baobab, only to find us all fenced out by the local authorities, the tree no longer in the public domain. Where did the troubled souls go now, I wondered? Was this a sad governmental attempt to push the local populace away from the treatments of traditional healers and into the ways of western medicine?

Still accessible though, at least in 2022, is the Great Baobab, which grows amongst the Swahili ruins at Mnarani on the Kenya coast. Behind the sign naming the tree was a small hole in which were clearly visible piles of crumpled papers. A plaque below explained how different traditional healers still incorporate the tree into their rituals, walking seven times round it with their patient, then posting a prayer into the slit in the tree before leaving without looking back.

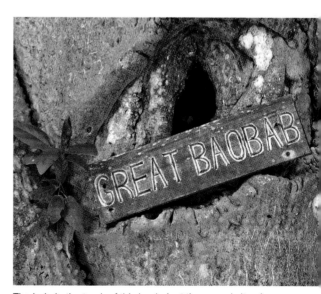

The hole in the trunk of this baobab at the sacred site of Mnarani on the Kenyan coast was filled with crumpled papers – prayers or maybe notes of thanks.

A tradition of healing

Traditional healing in Africa seldom distinguishes between treatment of mind or body, irrespective of which the sickness is apparently afflicting. Illness is seen as striking at both, or being caused by an imbalance of one manifesting itself in a disturbance of the other. To treat the body in isolation, as western allopathic medicine does, is almost inconceivable. Traditional treatment entails the prescription of medicine, but it places far greater stress on a psychological approach to its administration. Traditional healing is a more personal practice, with individual practitioners bringing to the medicine itself, or to its application, their own idiosyncratic contributions.

Nonetheless, the subjective nature of traditional treatment should not detract from the fundamental and well-accepted medicinal properties of various parts of different plants. Some of these properties are so widely recognized as to be common to the whole continent; others are confined to a single tribal area.

Any body of traditional medicinal knowledge has accumulated in many different ways, not least through a multi-generational process of trial, observation and maybe disastrous error before remedies finally received general acceptance. An awareness of some of the medicinal or nutritional benefits of baobab fruit may be inherited, even from our quadrupedal days. Other wisdom could have been received by shamans while in altered states of consciousness, and then handed down to practitioners of traditional healing.

Near Mtwara, in southern Tanzania, I talked with several *waganga* – a Swahili word for those who treat sickness with a combination of traditional medicinal remedies and psychological 'witchcraft'. They all prescribed a toothache treatment derived from baobab sap, and one of them advised his patients to rub themselves all over with a similar decoction to restore flagging vitality – a procedure he vividly enacted down to the removal of all his clothes except a pair of tartan underpants. Beyond this, the baobab had no medicinal properties of

Not only for export to the western world, baobab seeds and pith are also much consumed in Africa. Here they are being prepared in Zanzibar.

which any of them was aware, although the trees or their parts played an important role in the more ceremonial aspects of their craft.

Further north in Tanzania, many Hadzabe hunter-gatherers will say that they too have almost no medicinal use for any part of the baobab, other than the pulp, which they eat more as food than medicine. Not even their gods are connected with the trees, but rather the sun and the moon. The Hadzabe live impoverished lives, surviving exclusively on what they can gather from their environment, and their minimal use of the baobab's resources is astonishing. Elsewhere, particularly in West Africa, the position is dramatically different, and the lush chemical factory of the tree in full leaf is an irresistible source of nutritional, medicinal or spiritual benefit.

Arboreal pharmacy

The leaves alone are almost a panacea for the ills of the surrounding communities, with healers and mothers applying them to patients or children as emollients, tranquillizers and astringents. Rich in calcium and vitamin A, leaves also treat diarrhoea, dysentery, asthma, colic, eye infections, general fatigue, fever, inflammations, earache,

Above: Omar, the custodian of this baobab shrine on the Kenyan coast, would first consult with his visitors in an outside office, before bringing them here to be treated. **Right:** The pith surrounding baobab seeds is almost universally appreciated as a food and medicine wherever the trees grow; its vitamin C both prevents and cures disease.

kidney problems, urinary infections, insect bites, digestive and respiratory problems, excess sweating and tumours. They are used to treat malaria as well and as a prophylactic against the illness. Concoctions of powdered leaves are used as antihistamines, expectorants, and diaphoretics to promote sweating. Powdered leaves (*lalo*) are a staple in the diets of many West Africans, who believe these also help cleanse their blood.

External wounds are treated with leaf poultices, which are believed by northern Nigerians to help heal the wounds of circumcision. Livingstone cured skin ulcers with poultices of baobab leaf powder. These sores may have erupted through lack of vitamin C, and it is quite possible that once his expedition came across baobab trees, its members also ate the vitamin-rich pulp from the seed pod, thus stimulating the healing process from within.

The bark has a very bitter taste and was once used commercially for treating fevers, under the Latin name *cortex cael cedra* – 'heavenly blue bark'. A decoction is used to bathe children with rickets and other weaknesses, and added to steam baths to control shivering, colds and flu. Over much of the continent it makes a mouthwash for toothache sufferers, and in parts of Tanzania, boiled bark peelings are used to treat stomach ache and general body pains. A tasteless and insoluble gum can be extracted from the sap and applied to cleanse wounds and sores.

The oily red mush of pounded *Strophanthus* seeds is one of many lethal poisons with which the San and other hunters in southern Africa tip their arrows. Most poison users have developed an antidote to the lethal effects of their toxic arrow tips, and for the San this is found in baobab seeds. The active ingredient is an alkaloid, traces of which are also found in the bark. In Malawi it is juices from the trunk, rather than the seeds, that are smeared around the wounds of animals killed with poisoned arrows to neutralize the toxin before the kill is consumed.

In South Africa, many local people were said to use the powdered seeds to stop children hiccoughing, while both seeds and pulp treat dysentery in Central Africa. The seeds can also be ground into a paste for massaging onto sore teeth and gums, and in other parts of the continent, for easing gastric and kidney complaints, and aching joints. The paste may be swallowed or applied externally, and the Wakamba in Kenya first make incisions around the infected area before rubbing it into the skin.

The Senegalese island of Joal Fadiouth is remarkable for many reasons, not least for this Christian and Muslim cemetery, where the baobabs certainly predate the graves.

THE AFRICAN BAOBAB

THE HEALING TREE

The white pulp encasing the seeds treats malaria and other fevers, and is used to revive weakened children. Vitamin C is an aid to general good health, and it is easy to understand how soup or sauce made from the pulp would promote overall wellbeing, acting both to prevent and cure diseases. In some parts of Africa the pulp is used as a disinfectant, and in others as a dysentery treatment, while its use as a cure for measles and smallpox seems widespread.

Even roots have their uses, and can be soaked in water and used to bathe babies in order to strengthen their immune systems. Like other parts of the tree, powdered roots are said to make an effective treatment for malaria. Healers also apply concoctions containing baobab roots to relieve general lassitude, as well as impotence – alleviating the one no doubt going a long way towards curing the other.

The genesis of treatment

Theoretically, similar uses of the same raw materials in different parts of the world could derive from traditional practices inherited from a common ancestor. However, in many cases this idea raises far more questions than it answers. The Tanzanian Hadzabe have a very similar click language to that of the San in Namibia and Botswana, and both live hunter-gatherer lives around baobab trees. Yet while they may share distant ancestors, my hope of discovering they also share some particularly esoteric usage of baobab parts was not realized.

On the other hand, completely unrelated tribal groups, separated by several thousand miles of open savanna or tangled forest, sometimes reach similar ethnobotanical conclusions. The Wakamba are the only people in East Africa recorded as using juice from baobab leaves to cure infected eyes. In Senegal, young stems are crushed to provide a similar treatment. Local tribesfolk in parts of Kenya found that baobab roots made a good red dye, as they also did in Gambia.

Fundamentally, the most obvious way to gain knowledge is from others who already have it.

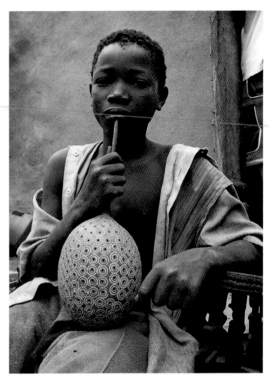

Intricately decorated baobab pods such as this one have a variety of ceremonial uses for the Dogon people in Mali.

Appreciation of the particular medicinal properties of plants is often regional rather than tribal, and unless there was a dramatic language barrier, it is likely that knowledge, however acquired, diffused into surrounding areas. The benefits accruing from eating pulp from the pod are known throughout the continent, and even the baobab bark toothache treatment is almost Africa-wide. Sometimes, though, knowledge seems strangely restricted. Are the Giriama the only ones to dig out pieces of the central tap root of younger trees to make a decoction with which to treat blood disorders? Why does smouldering pulp not keep insects off children's faces or leftover food in more of the continent than it does?

Just as the availability of alternatives regulates the importance of baobab leaves as a source of

THE AFRICAN BAOBAB

nourishment for humans or their livestock, so it must presumably affect the extent to which medicinal use is made of baobab parts. In *Useful Plants of Ghana*, Daniel Abbiw points to over 70 different herbal remedies for toothache, which can be gargled, chewed, swallowed, sucked, or made into ointments and mouthwashes. Baobab bark decoction is just one of the 70, which must speak loudly about the reliance on any one treatment diminishing in the face of available alternatives.

Madagascar's first human inhabitants may have arrived over 5 000 years ago, but to an ethnobotanically blank slate. Most of them came from the east, Polynesia or Malaya, where nothing like baobabs existed. Having no relationship with the island's bizarre vegetation, they must have relied initially on trial and error (or, perhaps, carefully studying the habits of wild animals) to discover what was good for them.

Hungry immigrants would quickly have discovered that the pulp of baobab fruit was both palatable and non-poisonous, even if its true nutritional worth took longer to appreciate, and now the fruit is a valuable supplement to a lot of impoverished diets of fish and rice. Being sailors, early settlers would also have wasted no time in searching for barks, vines and other rope-twisting fibres. How long was it before they started using the inner bark from the huge cylindrical trunks of *Adansonia grandidieri*? Recognizing the more abstruse medicinal properties of baobabs would have come less easily to the immigrants and in distant rural areas of Madagascar, the inhabitants may still be in the learning stage. There are very few records of any medicinal usage beyond the preparation from the bark of the very localized *A. suarezensis* as a treatment for diabetes.

Aboriginals have been in Australia far longer than anyone has inhabited Madagascar. This, and the scarcity of natural resources over much of the land they call home, seems to

With such limited distributions the Madagascar baobabs (here *Adansonia suarezensis* outside Diego Suarez) are much less used in traditional medicines than is the African species.

have fomented a deep affinity with the environment. Like almost anyone else around a baobab tree, Aboriginal Australians eat boab fruit pulp, either dry or mixed into a soup, and also make use of the seeds – raw, roasted, baked or ground into a paste. While Thomas Baines was in Australia in 1855 on the North Australia Exploring Expedition, he described curing scurvy by feeding sailors a jam of boab fruit and sugar, presumably a treatment grounded in Aboriginal practice. Baines also followed the indigenous inhabitants in chewing wood for its moisture. Feeding boab leaves to cattle, as Aboriginals do, mirrors the practice in the drier lands of Africa; so does stripping the inner bark fibres and, after pounding them with rocks, rolling them into lengths of string. Producing a sort of super-glue from boab pollen, strong enough to fix the metal heads to spear shafts, also has parallels in Africa.

Compared with the worldwide popularity of dried baobab pulp for disease prevention and general well-being, there is relatively little commercial exploitation of other baobab products for global medicinal use. Despite scientific research having endorsed many of the traditionally recognized properties of the tree's parts, quantities of active ingredients seem to be present in insufficient

Over most of its range, much more sustainable use could be made of the baobab; sheep and goats will greedily eat young leaves if these are harvested for them.

THE AFRICAN BAOBAB

quantities for fruit or leaves to be worth harvesting. Such medicinal benefits as the baobab might theoretically have to offer First World sufferers seem to be better extracted from other plants with more potent chemical make-ups.

Regardless of the ingredients in traditional herbal medicines, the ritual surrounding the treatment can be crucial to its success. This is epitomized in the practice of the East African *mganga* – they may be any combination of doctor, apothecary, priest, soothsayer, spirit medium, shaman, even magician or hypnotist, and treatments almost always combine elements of the psychological and physiological. The idea of transferring sickness, or using trees or other natural or personal objects as channels through which illness can be released, is a common component of traditional healing. In Tanzania I met a local Makonde with an open suppurating wound on his leg. He had eventually decided to visit the *mganga*. With much ceremony, the healer had massaged ointment all over the wound, and then, pulling a twig from out of his bag of talismans, had directed the limping patient to rub this around the wound. With the twig well soaked with juices from the sore, the patient was told to stick it into a baobab tree, which would then absorb the sickness.

It is probably impossible to dissociate the truly pharmacological benefits of traditional treatment from the psychological effects of the ceremony surrounding it. *Jinns* (*djinnis*, *jinnis* or genies) are spirits, sometimes evil and often inspired by fertile – and fearful – imaginations. Traditional doctors can influence these imaginations, perhaps by embroidering the existence of jinns to such an extent that the medicinal treatment becomes almost irrelevant compared to the manipulations of the mind.

Infertile women can be cruelly stigmatized in African society, and their problems account for a large part of any *mganga's* business. When visited by a patient for the first time, a traditional Wakamba healer may shake a gourd full of rattling trinkets. If seven baobab seeds tumble out onto the earthen floor of the hut, the patient – man or woman – is seen to be under a spell preventing him or her from having children. To lift the spell, the doctor takes baobab fibre rope, anoints it with a combination of powders and potions, and ties seven knots along its length. He then holds the rope over the patient's head and pulls hard on each end, undoing the knots. Fertility is then assured. This may be one man's treatment, but inevitably one is left wondering whether any of it is common to other healers, or whether it is entirely the fruit of his own inventiveness or imagination.

Some years ago, I talked to an old Makonde medicine man called Mayunga. He was happy to discuss his practice – but only after being presented with clothes or bags of fruit. After talking through our interpreter (the local teacher) for half an hour, he started slowing down and the answers came with increasing reluctance. This was not, I was told, because he was tired, but rather that I had exhausted the worth of my gifts, and he expected more if he was to continue disclosing his secrets. Mayunga was like a jukebox that needed feeding with money to get music, but his music was sweet. His particular baobab shrine of healing was in the middle of a sisal plantation. He would give patients a clay pot full of medicine and direct them to the tree. There they should empty the contents over their naked bodies, alone, before smashing the pot at their feet. When I visited the tree, shards of broken pots littered the ground, in fine testament to his popularity as a healer.

Richest of all Mayunga's stories, worth bags more avocados than I had with me, was the revelation of his supernatural powers. As a youth working on a Tanzanian sisal plantation, he was told one day to cut down a baobab. He spent six hours chopping away at the tree knowing it would take three days to fell. Next day he returned to his work, only to find an untouched trunk, showing no signs of the previous day's damage. Once more Mayunga set to, piles of wood chips slowly

In some cultures felling a baobab is inconceivable, for fear of dislodging the spirits that live there, but these Wakamba in Kenya were happy to sacrifice the tree for more building space.

collecting at his feet as he hacked his way round the spongy bole. The following morning he again found the baobab unharmed and entire, so he went and told his employer that he neither would nor could cut down the tree. Unsurprisingly he was sacked, and the job given to his brother, Alambalamba, who duly toppled the giant, but immediately fell very sick. The Makonde have long believed that cutting down a baobab will make your neck stiffen rigidly at right angles, which was just what happened to Alambalamba. Mayunga visited his brother and felt as soon as he walked into the darkened room that he would be able to loosen his neck, which he did. This first recognition of his own spiritual strength he attributed to the tree he could not kill, and he has revered baobabs ever since.

Today, many herbal medicines are sold from conventional pharmacies to be taken without any particular ceremony. Always critical to a medicine's success in healing is the patient's confidence in the treatment. Men who become strong and virile from drinking water mixed with baobab sap do so through the strength of their belief in the remedy as much as because of the medical properties of the tree. However, in South Africa, babies too young to formulate such notions are washed in the mixture to strengthen their immunity, so its efficacy must rely on something other than any psychological impact of the treatment on the patient. West African fishermen rinse themselves down with an infusion of baobab seeds to protect against crocodile attacks. This presumably induces a crocodile-repelling aroma in the skin, which could perhaps be scientifically identified. Still, one should not deride the notion that beliefs can be strong enough to influence not only the believers, but also the behaviour of animals or other people with whom they interact.

Sacred trees and spirits

While trees often become focal points for public prayer and healing, seldom are they formally consecrated as places of worship as is a baobab at Keren, a beautiful mountain-ringed town in northern Eritrea. There, in 1881, a hollow baobab was dedicated as a shrine to St Mariam of Dearit. Other than on the 29th of May each year, when thousands of celebrating pilgrims descend on the town, the shrine is a peaceful place, approached along an avenue of neem trees. The statue of the Virgin Mary within the empty baobab trunk is unusual for her blackness. As refuges and homes for so many wild creatures, hollow baobabs also shelter humans all over Africa and, while Allied forces bombarded Keren from the surrounding mountains in World War II, Italian soldiers took refuge in this baobab shrine. What are described as shrapnel marks are still visible today. The tree's subsequent adoption by the Roman Catholic church seems to have

The Shrine of St Mariam of Dearit in Eritrea may have saved the lives of Italian soldiers who sheltered there during a World War II bombardment of the town of Keren. This picture was taken some 20 years ago, and the surrounds of the shrine are now much more developed to accommodate the increased number of visitors.

The statue of the Virgin Mary inside the consecrated baobab in Keren, Eritrea.

beliefs of Arabs better blurred than in a grove of baobabs round an old Islamic town.

Some sacred sites, like the baobab on the Dar es Salaam waterfront once was, are taken over as trees of prayer and healing for the whole community. Others are the precincts of individual traditional doctors who may invoke help from spirits living in the tree or else summoned from further afield to give their assistance. Recognition of particular spirits may be confined to the minds of single communicants; otherwise several visitors may share similar experiences. I naively asked a healer in Mombasa how it happened that so many of her patients offered similar descriptions of a particular spirit, and, with a wave of her hand at the nearby tree, she replied simply, 'Because it's there'.

An hour's drive north of Mombasa is Kilifi Creek, its south side edged by low cliffs of fossilized coral, above which are the grasslands and sisal fields of Kilifi Plantations. When supervising bush clearing one day, the farm's owner asked his foreman to be sure to preserve any young baobabs. The immediate response was that baobabs were seldom cut down anyway, as they were the resting place of *jinns*. The foreman then pointed to a young sapling, growing far out on its own, adding that no one would ever cut that one down because its spirits had too far to jump to reach the next baobab, and so would possess its destroyer instead.

The foreman was a Giriama, who believe strongly that spirits, more usually bad ones, occupy hollow baobabs. Village entrances are often sited under baobab branches so that anyone arriving with evil intentions will either be recognized and disarmed by the tree spirits, or will abandon any bad spirits to the tree on passing underneath it. During the construction of one of the causeways linking Mombasa Island to the mainland, construction workers refused to cut down a baobab blocking the designated route. No one, they contended, could order them to do something that would arouse such anger in the tree's occupying spirits; the causeway had to be rerouted or they would stop work. Colonial

enhanced its appeal to anyone in need of spiritual revitalization, and many of its visitors go there for the sanctity and tranquility of the place, as much as for its Christianity.

All along the East African coast the spiritual beliefs of Africa's indigenous people have become interwoven with the tenets of Arab immigrants. Old mosques and tombs may be relics of the Islamic tradition, but the power of their past is strong enough to attract people of any religious or animist persuasion. They, and the trees that surround them, create a vital link between the living and the dead.

While Muslims once worshipped at the mosques, the trees overshadowing their ruins may now house the spirits of the ancestors of African animists, who still come to commune with these spirits. Nowhere are the edges between the animist spirituality of indigenous Africans and the Islamic

THE AFRICAN BAOBAB

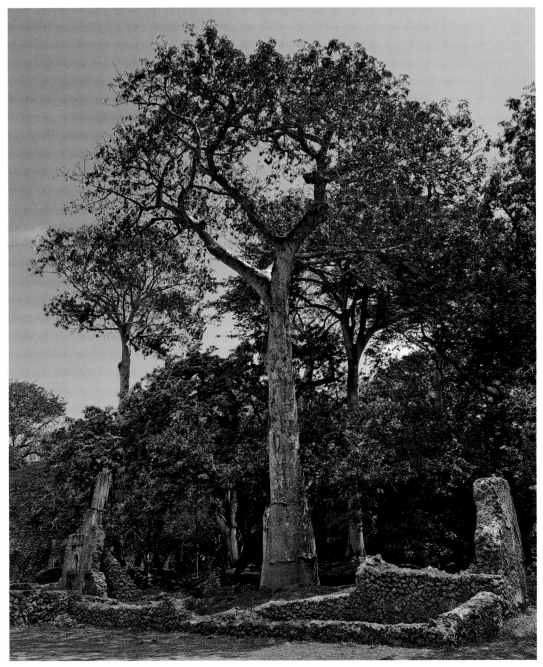

Baobabs growing around abandoned Islamic settlements may also be significant for the animist cultures along the East African coast (this is Gedi, near Malindi in Kenya). The trees may even mark the sites of ancient graves.

administrators countered with the argument that the Government Spirit was far more powerful than the Baobab Spirit, and it would never lower itself to living in a tree. 'Seven days to quit' said a notice pinned to the baobab one morning, signed 'The Government Spirit'. On day eight the tree was felled.

However sacred trees may be, there is usually a way of bargaining with the spirits or appeasing the gods, so that the mighty giants of forest or savanna can be felled without fear of recrimination. Sometimes trees – or fish or mammals – must die so that the tribe can survive, and the prayers before a tree is felled meld apology and appeasement with reverence and respect. This is no contradiction. When water began backing up behind Zambia and Zimbabwe's Kariba Dam, spirits inhabiting the doomed baobabs were successfully relocated, first by a ceremony of prayer and ritual, followed by the tying of branches from trees to be flooded onto others above the full water line.

Despite their otherworldliness, some gods and spirits are thought to require incentive or reward on Earth in exchange for their interventions, and the base of sacred trees may be heaped with offerings. Bottles, coconut husks, or the shells of large land snails laid at the bottom of a tree have usually held traditional alcohol, rose water or other symbolic liquids. Articles of clothing, once worn by the supplicant, may be left behind, perhaps in an attempt to shift sickness from the wearer to the tree, and then even onto another person. Occasionally money is offered up, presumably symbolically rather than in any real belief that good health or fertility actually has a price.

The first time I explored a sacred baobab near Kilifi, a pile of five- and ten-cent coins lay beside it. On my next visit to the tree, a few months later, the money was gone. So, I said to myself, was the thief either so desperate he was prepared to risk incurable madness – the price of stealing from a shrine – for a few cents, or was he otherwise sure of the superior strength of his own juju? Then I became ashamed of such thoughts, and determined to

accept that the healing spirit had simply collected its dues – that was better. Anyway, gifts of food or drink are meant to be shared with God or the resident spirits, and their disappearance from the foot of the tree is a sign that prayers have been heard.

In what was then the Baobab Café, underneath a fine old baobab in old Stone Town in Zanzibar, I met Fatma, a powerful Swahili woman who had lived in and around Stone Town for much of her life. She recalled this tree looming large over her childhood.

As a growing child, Fatma, together with her friends, would stop and play under the café's baobab, innocently searching for fallen fruit or flowers. When she reached puberty, her mother told Fatma that a bad spirit lived in the tree, which

Was the act of pinning this scarf to a baobab trunk a plea for help, or a token of thanks for prayers answered? Could it have been pinned there during a healing ritual, or did someone simply bring their troubles and the scarf to the tree of their own accord?

THE AFRICAN BAOBAB

preyed upon young girls, never leaving once it had haunted them. Suitably alarmed, Fatma devised a different route home, avoiding the tree. Many years later she began wondering why her mother had not mentioned the evil spirit earlier in her life. Why was she, Fatma, one of very few children who knew anything about it anyway? With neither parent alive to ask, she had concluded that her mother wanted to stop her hanging around with boys by frightening her into finding a new way home. It would also not have escaped her mother that the tree was very close to the Persian Baths and on the days reserved for men, unsavoury characters would loiter around the cafe.

Despite or even because of the nature of its spiritual occupants, there is great serenity beneath the spreading branches of a huge baobab tree. Is it only shade that brings that feeling of rest and relief, or is there something more? Have the elephants that once sheltered there from the midday sun or gouged away trunkfuls of moisture-laden fibre left behind some invisible reminders of their passing? Do vestiges of countless disputes settled by tribal elders still linger under the trees to help newcomers resolve their own differences? So many supplicants bringing the cares of the world to the base of a baobab must surely confer on that tree an aura of spiritual hope and expectation. Many baobabs have been around much longer than the great Christian cathedrals of northern Europe, and plenty of these trees have also served as places of worship. There is no escaping the incomparable sensation of stillness and tranquility within an old church. It would be strange if similar feelings did not pervade the shade of ancient baobab trees.

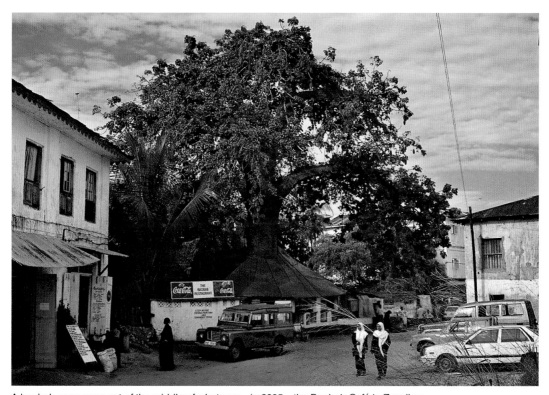

A baobab once grew out of the middle of what was – in 2005 – the Baobab Café in Zanzibar.

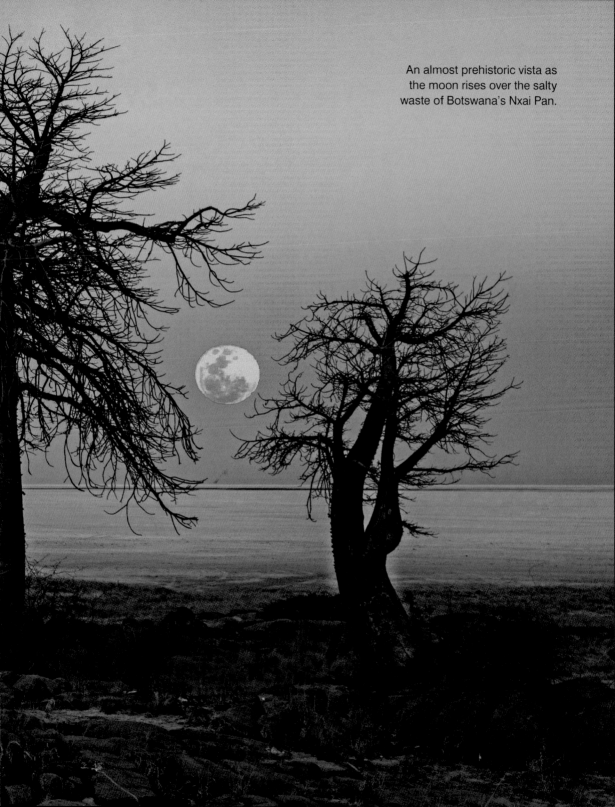

An almost prehistoric vista as
the moon rises over the salty
waste of Botswana's Nxai Pan.

CHAPTER NINE

The baobab's destiny

'No longer is it acceptable to set aside great swaths of wild land for conservation, to the exclusion of all human beings. Now development is as inevitable in Africa as it is elsewhere, and one can only hope it is undertaken sensitively, minimising both social and environmental upheaval. Be that as it may, the destruction of mature trees is one of the inevitable consequences of almost any change in the use of previously untouched countryside.'

These baobabs have been spared, with the ground nuts having been sown right up to the edge of the trunks. From the lopped look of the trees, this is clearly a West African scene (actually Senegal) but as in so many other parts of the continent, one cannot help but wonder how the next generation of baobabs will ever get going.

THE AFRICAN BAOBAB

Felling a giant

Of the many unplanned setbacks contributing to the failure of the Tanganyika Groundnut Scheme, one of the first was the difficulty of converting thick African bush into peanut-growing plains. At Kongwa, baobabs posed the biggest problem. These ancient trees were pushed by giant earth-movers, pulled by wheeled tractors, and even dynamited in an effort to complete the desolation and ensure nothing interrupted the military straightness of the crop lines. Only after a bulldozer dislodged a human skull from one of the trees did the Administration begin appreciating that the trees meant more to the local people than somewhere to hang a beehive or take refuge from the sun. In the end, however, what saved a pitiful scattering of the trees was not a sudden appreciation of their cultural, spiritual or aesthetic values, but rather the simple realization that they took up less space alive than felled.

A distant lone baobab survived the wanton 1947 clearance of Tanganyikan bush in the course of the disastrous Groundnut Scheme.

The destruction of baobabs was also one of the prices paid for the conversion of lowland East African scrub into plantations of sisal, although even today some of these host large numbers of very big trees, clearly far older than the plantations. In West Africa and Sudan, baobabs came under threat because their wrinkled bark or fallen seed pods created refuges for insects that were harmful to cocoa or cotton crops. Mealy bugs spread viruses from baobabs to cocoa trees, while stainer bugs damaged cotton bolls in their search for oil in the seeds.

Localized felling of trees is inevitable when they block roads, airstrips, railways, electricity lines, mines, dams and other development. Seldom, though, is the desecration of baobabs so complete as to change the landscape forever. Planting sisal, cotton, cocoa and other crops has taken its toll, but the Groundnut Scheme probably represented the greatest attempt ever to rub the baobab tree off a corner of its distribution map.

In urban areas, big baobabs are easily assimilated into the everyday life of residents, who may make good use of the tree trunk, particularly if it is hollow. However, if more space is needed for houses or shops, or unscrupulous developers see profit from a treeless plot, then trees may go. A huge baobab in Malindi on the Kenyan coast is so revered as to have its own name – *Mbuyu Wa Kusema* – the Whispering Tree. This seems to refer not only to the sound of leaves rustling in

When the developer has finally cut down the last trunk of the Whispering Tree in Malindi, where then will the local people go to say their prayers?

THE AFRICAN BAOBAB

the wind, but also to its function as an arboreal confessional, where locals quietly and privately unburden their problems – or did. When I visited in late 2022, almost half the bulk of the tree had been felled by a private developer, and the rest looked sure to follow. Where will people whisper now? In agricultural areas, small-scale cultivators usually spare baobabs, and the trees stand on as forlorn reminders of nature's original mosaic. As land is passed from one generation to the next, and each successor inherits a smaller plot, the all-consuming baobabs are seen as taking up increasingly

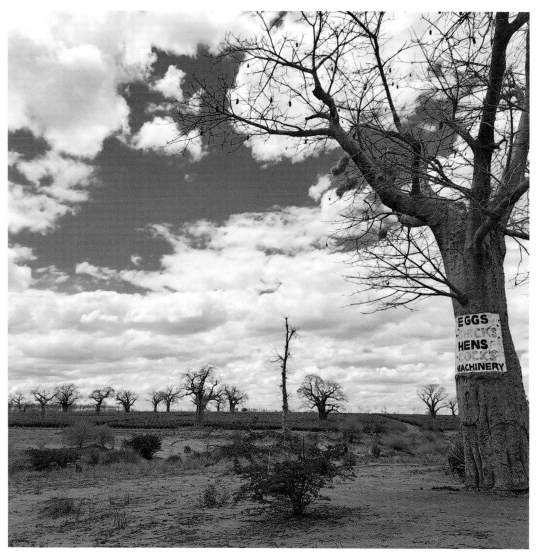

Hardly any of the baobabs were destroyed during the planting up of this Kenyan sisal estate. If livestock is kept out, young trees might have a chance to establish themselves between the rows of sisal plants.

THE BAOBAB'S DESTINY

The incorporation of baobabs in contemporary art cannot help but raise general awareness of the trees.

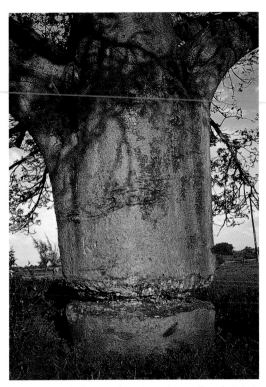

This tree was being cut down to make way for a hut, but was spared at the last minute by the intervention of the local chief; several years on, it shows no ill effects from the gaping wound all round its trunk.

valuable space. If they must be cut down, they will be, without compunction. I would love to think of the baobab tree as a pan-African symbol of resilience, a resting place for ancestral spirits, and a sacred source of strength and inspiration. Sadly, though, this would be romanticizing the truth. Yes, the baobab's public profile is certainly on the up, not only where the trees grow, but also in urban areas, far from their natural habitat. However, throughout much of the continent the baobab is spared – not only because it is hard to destroy, spiritually revered or a source of palatable fruit, but because the moist wood is unsuitable as building material, charcoal or firewood and the trees occupy more surface area when felled, at least until they rot away.

There are many economic arguments both for and against leaving baobabs standing on cultivated land, making it near impossible to arrive at irrefutable conclusions as to their net worth. The trees take up space that other plants could otherwise occupy. They reduce solar light and rainfall by about half underneath the spread of their branches, and bring down soil temperatures by several degrees. On the other hand, water content in soil is higher in open land immediately after the start of rainy seasons, but it remains damper longer under the trees once rains have stopped. There are also more nutrients in the areas around the trees than out in the open.

The two-day demolition of a 1 000-year-old creation cannot seem other than a tragedy, both

THE AFRICAN BAOBAB

for its species as well as for humanity. Perhaps worse is the destruction of younger established trees, their huge potential to nourish the surrounding community as yet unfulfilled. Nonetheless, the real danger to the baobab's future comes much more from the destruction of seedlings, or of habitat that would otherwise support them. Today, there is hardly an acre of African savanna outside national parks and reserves where too many domestic animals are not searching for too little grazing. Even within protected areas, game is often artificially confined by the closure of old dispersal routes, with similar effect. So, the seedlings and small trees that should eventually replace the great old landmarks find themselves victims of their own palatability.

While the baobabs' preferred environment is on the dry side of average for African bush country, it may be well-enough watered for its human inhabitants to imagine they can grow crops there. These people are often one-time pastoralists whose wanderings have gradually become restricted in the same way as those of the wild animals, their plight exacerbated by changes in climate or government policies and the subdivision of large tracts of communally held land into privately owned plots. Inevitably, the natural vegetation is then replaced with sorghum, millet, okra, and sometimes maize. Even if these crops fail, the land will be grazed to the ground and baobabs are unlikely ever to grow there again.

These photographs show the same tree, the one on the right taken a year or so after the one on the left. In the interim, the baobab's top has been grazed off by elephants in search of dry-season food – something that must, ultimately, affect the shape of the mature tree.

Where is the next generation?

During my researches for this book, I counted and measured baobabs within two radically different areas of Kenya. The first survey was conducted on the lands of Kilifi Plantations, where many of the 1 200 baobabs we measured dominate permanent grass paddocks. Grazing by the dairy herd effectively ensures that the only seeds with any chance of growing into trees are those germinating in strips and gullies of uncultivated land beyond the pasture fences. The other survey was undertaken near Kibwezi, midway between Mombasa and Nairobi. The area is relatively recently settled, and most of the big trees have been left in the fields, with small belts of natural riparian vegetation remaining along the stream beds.

What emerged from both studies, with startling clarity, was a frightening dearth of very young trees. There were about as many very young as very old trees, when there should have been a massive natural surplus of young over older members of the species.

In addition to the destructive attentions of goats, gazelles or dairy herds, and the insidious shrinkage of their range because of human interference, baobabs may be feeling the heat of brush fires. Big baobabs, with their pachydermal skins, moisture-laden wood and amazing powers of recovery, can easily live on through fires inflaming the surrounding scrub. However, deliberate burning of dead grass before each rainy season gives young seedlings little chance to attain the critical height and degree of resistance to survive the next fire.

No matter how respected and conserved the mature trees may be, relentless grazing pressure will not give young ones any chance of surviving.

THE AFRICAN BAOBAB

Lack of recruitment; where is the next generation? These themes recur in scientific surveys and in journeys through baobab country. Even allowing for the inevitable difficulty in finding young baobabs, the signs of young trees are disturbingly hard to discern. S M Venter and E T F Witkowski asked the same question in their paper, 'Where are the young baobabs?' They studied the trees in an enclosed southern African plot, concluding that the increase in the natural baobab population was minimal without any livestock in the enclosure, and non-existent once goats got in to browse.

The Kenyan Forestry Research Institute on the Nairobi–Mombasa road once offered free indigenous trees to local farmers. Among the assorted species were baobabs, neatly packaged in pots made from half a pod of their own fruit. Given the choice, farmers usually rejected the offer of a free baobab, almost as though fearing invasion by unwelcome spirits, but in truth because they perceived the trees as useless. If they really believed baobabs have been around 'since Noah's time', as a Wakamba woman once told me, perhaps they also considered that any benefit a young tree might eventually confer was too remote to contemplate.

Some 500 years ago, the Dogon people arrived at the bottom of the cliffs forming the Bandiagara Escarpment in Mali, driving out the Tellem tribe, which then inhabited the area. The Dogon were probably responding to the spread of Islam around the edges of their ancestral territories, as well as to the slave raids from which the cliffs of their new home offered protection. The floodplains below the cliffs also provided fertile ground for crops, and it is said the Dogon were led there by a huge serpent that also showed them streams, waterfalls, and the many uses of the baobab tree.

So humanity depended on tree, and this in itself ensured the baobab's future, at least until the early 20th century, when the spread of European influence began to unbalance the continent. The Dogon are still there today, as are the *oro* (baobabs), which have provided a stable source of wild food ever since the invaders' arrival. However, populations of both Dogon and their livestock are expanding dramatically, income from tourism is almost non-existent, and competition for dwindling natural resources is unrelenting. The desert is encroaching fast and now there is almost nothing but sand dunes beyond the floodplains.

Every picture tells a story; here, a couple of hunter-gatherers lament the destruction of a young baobab, felled by immigrant pastoralists (with no ancestral connection to this environment) so its leaves could be fed to their livestock.

THE AFRICAN BAOBAB

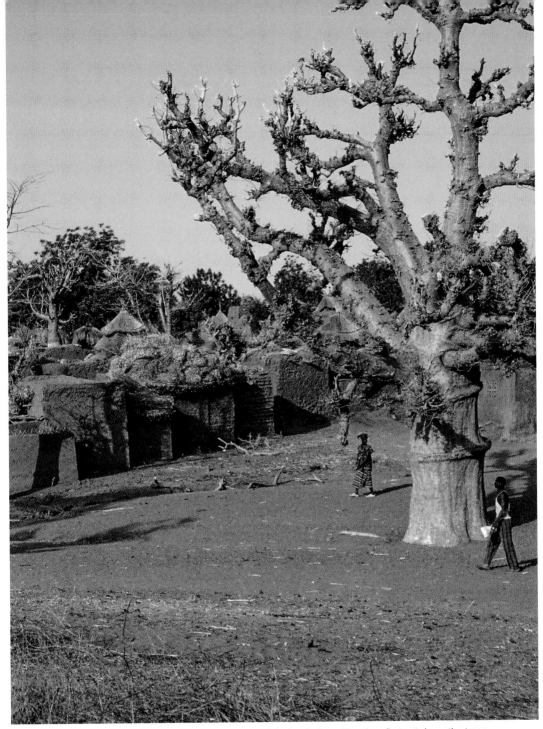

The Dogon of Mali would always build their villages round the baobabs, rather than first cut down the trees.

THE BAOBAB'S DESTINY

The modern advantages of communication and travel are slowly severing the bonds that bind people to their immediate environment. With Africa's ever-expanding population, areas of land need to support increasing numbers of human inhabitants and their animal dependants. Once an area is full, people move on to other land with which they have no ancestral connection at all. This was evident as we researched the baobabs in Kibwezi, an area settled in the 1960s by Wakamba from far away, where no baobabs grew. Arriving with no spiritual, ethnobotanical or nutritional experience of the trees, the only value they could place on them was nuisance. If the trees were too much work to cut down, they were certainly not worth replacing when they eventually toppled over. The same scenario applied to the Hadzabe, whose traditional Tanzanian homelands were being squeezed on all sides by onion farmers, conservationists, and incoming pastoralists with little understanding of, and no connection to, their new environment.

The sense of permanence that once joined successive generations to the same area of land is slowly disintegrating. As a result, the responsibility of land stewardship for the next generation is vanishing. In its place is the notion of absolute ownership, which implies a right to exploit the natural environment for the present with no thought for the future. The traditional ties that bound a community together are continually being loosened, and unless there is a personal and present benefit from planting trees, there is little incentive to do so.

At the same time, the animist credo linking individuals with their environment, through the belief that trees and animals harbour their own spirits, is disappearing. As a result, the protection afforded these natural spiritual resting places has also disappeared. Abandoned animist beliefs may perhaps be replaced by an adherence to conventional religions, but in most of these nature plays a relatively insignificant role.

Natural regeneration depends not only on wise management of the land where the trees might grow, but also on the continued attentions of pollinators and seed-dispersers. Bats still seem to be doing their night-time work, as they are able to adapt to life in and around human habitations. Seed-dispersers are faring less well. While the all-important baboons manage to survive on rocky hillsides, their presence is scarcely compatible with subsistence farming, and crop-raiding monkeys find it increasingly difficult to forage successfully.

THE AFRICAN BAOBAB

This tree is growing out of a low cliff and is older than its size suggests. Many years ago, when more baobabs grew around this end of Lake Manyara in Tanzania, baboons probably deposited the seed from which it emerged.

Tanzania's Lake Manyara is a soda lake at the foot of the escarpment up which slants the road to the Serengeti. Down towards the south end of the lake is a hot spring, Maji Moto, or 'hot water' in Swahili. Above the spring is a jumble of rocks, and a single, gnarled little baobab leans out over the lake edge, its roots scarcely distinguishable from the stone surfaces over which they snake. I watched a party of buffalo graze contentedly on the lush grass all around the spring, backed by pink clusters of flamingos filtering algae along the lake edge. It was an idyllic African landscape, although one with no other visible baobabs for many kilometres in any direction. Perhaps a few hundred years ago baboons dropped seeds there, one of which grew into that twisted, rock-clinging baobab. But where are the other descendants of the trees on whose seeds those baboons feasted during their lifetime?

THE BAOBAB'S DESTINY

So long as baboons thrive where baobabs grow, there remains the chance of seeds reaching rocky areas where any young trees will be less grazed.

Breeding and transplanting trees

Given the soaring demand for baobab products within and outside Africa, it is not surprising that individuals and institutions are trying to coax as many shoots as they can out of the dark brown seeds. As early as 1764, the seventh edition of *Miller's Gardener's Dictionary* gave advice on propagating baobabs in England, where they were 'too tender to thrive in this Country without this artificial Heat, therefore they must constantly remain in the Stove with other exotic Plants'.

Breeding trees is not the work for anyone in a hurry, particularly where baobabs are concerned. Having selected the preferred seeds, the next problem is to get as many of these to germinate as possible. A variety of treatments can improve the odds, the preferred one involving soaking the seeds in sulphuric acid. This was not a method I tried when I did my own propagation experiments, under the guidance of the computerized database from the International Centre for Research in Agroforestry. Their data informed me that after suitable pre-treatment, seeds may take as little as six days to germinate, and that germination success rate is usually 90–100%.

I began by planting five batches of 100 seeds, each in separate boxes. One batch was planted straight from a newly fallen pod, and another from the perfect environment of a cracked pod, into which invading insects had introduced damp soil. The third batch was covered with boiling water and soaked for 24 hours before planting, and all those in the fourth were first lightly cracked with pliers. I had painstakingly picked the remaining 100 seeds from baboon faeces beside the Athi River. After ten months, two shoots had appeared from these 500 seeds. Both died, and it was little consolation to read that experiments at the Royal Botanic Gardens in Kew had been even less successful.

Baobabs in nature may take 20 to 30 years to mature, which, however great the rewards at the

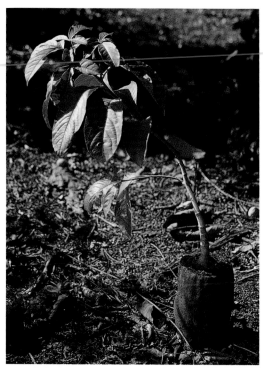

Perhaps some African farmers think that any benefits baobabs may eventually bestow are just too many years away to make them worthwhile planting. There were no takers for baobabs at this indigenous tree nursery in Kenya, even though they were being given away.

end, is far longer than any farmer is prepared to wait for his first dividend. So, once seeds have germinated, the next challenge is how best to nurture them to an early first crop of fruit. Two Ghanaian scientists have published a wonderfully optimistic paper 'Prospects of raising baobab to fruiting in two years', outlining their experiments that were aimed at reassuring farmers, who might otherwise be 'put off by the long maturity period of the plant'. Nurturing seeds to germinate was less of a problem than hastening young plants to maturity, which seemed best achieved by striking cuttings or grafting shoots onto older rootstock, rather than planting out seedlings. Hopefully their findings will provide the basis for more research.

THE AFRICAN BAOBAB

Somewhat surprisingly, baobabs can be transplanted easily much later in life, and anyone wishing to reinforce their belief in these trees being born big overnight should have been in Kasane in northern Botswana one day in 1995. In 1993 lightning struck the Mowana Hotel, as it was then known, and with it burnt the eponymous baobab ('mowana' in the local language). If the rebuilt hotel was to keep its name, it had to have a baobab. How? Simply dig up a big tree, lift it with a crane onto a low loader, and install it in the middle of the courtyard. The substitute now looks to have lived there all its life and is so large that the outstretched arms of five grown adults could barely encircle its trunk. Some years later, a team from De Beers Venetia Diamond Mine in Musina, South Africa, translocated a baobab at least as tall as the crane that lifted it. The mine's publicity material relates how it has relocated a total of 110 baobabs since 2008, and stresses how the trees will 'only take root in their new home if their trunks are planted facing precisely the same direction as in their original home'. But these translocation efforts are surpassed by those of the developers of the Palace of the Lost City resort (formerly Sun City) northwest of Johannesburg, which boasts of having transplanted 380 mature baobabs in order to create a 'baobab forest'.

More recently, a group of Kenyan intermediaries representing investors from Georgia, Eastern Europe, paid for and uprooted eight enormous standing baobabs from coastal farmers, who willingly sold the trees, which were taking up good agricultural space. It seems that all the necessary permits were obtained, but after a loud outcry from many residents, as well as allegations of 'biopiracy' from conservationists, the Kenyan president ordered an investigation into the export, which caused all involved authorities to backtrack. Despite the finding that all due process was satisfied, parliament then got involved, other NGOs brought more court cases, and after so many months out of their ancestral ground, lying desiccating on custom-built cradles, the trees are unlikely to survive in the Shekvetili Dendrological Park on the coast of the Black Sea.

This tree was uprooted with a view to its being exported from Kenya to Georgia on the Black Sea.

Enduring trees

Baobabs cast their shadows over a continent in transition, where huts give way to houses, horses to horsepower, dirt trails to tarred highways. While the trees stand witness to many hundreds of years of human behaviour, they leave no trace of their own passing, being poor subjects for fossilization, and drying to dust soon after their roots have finally ceased to channel water. The living trees speak for the species, while their remains cannot.

Today, the speed of environmental change is such that those plants and animals slow to adapt may be left behind on some ecological scrapheap – doomed relics of a former age. It is far too soon to commission a 'Requiem for the Baobab', or to start ensuring that the species is represented in every tropical city's botanical garden.

It is impossible to think of baobabs as remotely endangered, as they are spread so prominently over such a wide area. Nonetheless, droughts, overgrazing and land clearing are taking a relentless toll. If baobabs cannot adapt, the descendants of today's trees may be left to try and find rootholds in rocky clefts, fossilized coral, and any other places where hungry herbivores fear to tread.

In 200 years' time, most of the African landscape presently dominated by baobabs will look very different. Will wild baobabs in natural settings, like most of the continent's large mammals, then only be experienced in enclosed little pockets of protected land?

It is too easy, and almost *de rigueur*, to end any conservation story on a note of alarm, and enough warning bells have already been rung.

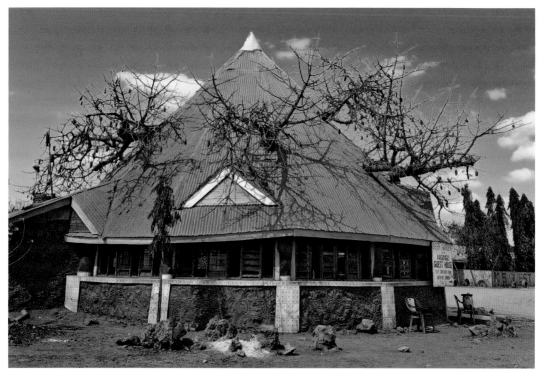

Whether the baobab was incorporated into the reception area of this Kenyan hotel in the name of artistic curiosity or genuine respect, it should still encourage visitors and maybe other builders to spare the trees.

THE AFRICAN BAOBAB

Will our descendants still be gazing at such majestic trees in 200 years' time?

Perhaps the best-known grove of baobabs in the whole of Africa is that known as Baines' Baobabs, growing on a tiny islet in Botswana's Kidiakam Pan, a salty lake-bed dry for ten months a year. Thomas Baines painted the trees in May 1862. The baobabs have been visited many times since by those keen to compare the living trees with their painted depiction, and by this author several years ago. Typical of baobabs on the edges of Botswana's dried pans, these ones showed themselves from far away as the tallest feature in the landscape. The sun had almost set and the trees had to compete for attention with a dozen elephants splashing around in a muddy pool of three-day-old rainwater. Reaching the trees entailed skirting round the edge of a dried saltpan across which hundreds of wildebeest and zebra were making their seemingly aimless way. Their hooves crunched on the cracked surface, belying the soft mud below. Most of Baines' baobabs are still there, just as they were painted over a century ago and, more importantly, so are lots of young ones. Even the fallen giant that had so intrigued Baines was putting out leafy shoots. A barn owl flew silently around the trees, and it was still light enough for this to set smaller birds, settling down to roost, into an agitated twitter. Squeaks came from the owl's abode, young ones perhaps, and maybe even descended from forebears that swooped around the fire while Thomas Baines laid his bearded head on whatever passed for a pillow. When the last of these huge historic trees has sucked up its final drop of water, to be remembered only in paintings, photographs and commemorative postage stamps, the young trees will have grown up to take the place of their famous ancestors, and a clump of baobabs will still break the distant horizon.

Baines' Baobabs, in Botswana, are seldom photographed with water around their island, not least because of the difficulty in reaching them in the rainy season.

Acknowledgements

Baobabs have loomed especially large over my life ever since I hiked along the bottom of the Dogon Escarpment in Mali, over 20 years ago. Despite having lived in East Africa for nearly half a century, with the nearest naturally growing baobab two-and-a-half hours' drive away from Nairobi, only in Mali did I begin to appreciate how vital these trees can sometimes be to the people living around them.

I started the first edition of this book soon after my return to Kenya from West Africa. Since publication of *The African Baobab* in 2007, I have continued to marvel at the wonders of baobab trees in many parts of this extraordinary continent. These experiences, my researches and the time spent writing and updating this work, have inspired a much better understanding of both tree ecology and the relationship between trees and people.

I must reiterate that if Malcolm Linton and Linda de Souza had not lived in Abidjan, Côte d'Ivoire, so providing a reason to visit West Africa and a base from which to reach Mali, it is highly unlikely this book would ever have been written – thank you both for being the catalyst for its creation.

A lot of other people helped me with the first edition in different ways, and I repeat, without mentioning them all again, how grateful I remain for their input as I foundered my way around so much unfamiliar botanical territory. Now I know more, but in the preparation of this edition, have still felt the need to draw on the knowledge of others and to ask for help in different ways.

In Kenya many friends gave information, pictures, company and hospitality, which all contributed in one way or another to my finalizing this work. Christopher Wilson and Betty Bundotich looked after me in Kilifi, and are still prepared to have me roaming all over Kilifi Plantations for my ongoing research. Susie Allan continued to be a source of general botanical help, as did Quentin Luke. I must thank Jim Birnie for reminding me how to find the baobabs in the Nairobi Arboretum, and David Taylor, Dudley Lucas and Peter Bateman, among others, for providing information on the often-confusing story about the attempted export of Kenyan trees to Georgia. Others down in baobab territory who helped included Bea Andersen, Betty Archer, Lissa Ruben, Sammy Katisho and Abigail Church, also Tom Lawrence, who willingly tidied up my story of the sniper in the tree in Taveta.

Outside Kenya, Len Newton, erstwhile Kenyan professor of botany now living in England, was just as much help as he was when he lived here. In America, David Baum – who continues to publish papers on *Adansonia* and probably knows more about the genus as a whole than anyone else on Earth – particularly helped by introducing me to one of his colleagues in South Africa, Diana Mayne. At the time of writing, I have yet to meet you Diana, but I must thank you most sincerely for being such a willing answerer of questions and fount of information – as indeed one might expect of someone with an email address including 'baobab' in it. More recently I met Sarah Venter, who is also a South African baobab professional, and has given me much help and advice along my way.

Many friends offered illustrations, some of which have appeared in this book, and whether they have featured or not, thanks to all of you for sharing these and for often going to considerable trouble to get them to me. Dudley Lucas took pictures of transplanting trees; Don Young put me in touch with Simon Keynes, who provided the illustration of David Livingstone's monogram; while Teddy Kinyanjui was always on the look-out for interesting trees in his travels through East Africa.

Out of Africa, I bugged various friends for pictures, including Carol Beckwith in England, Ali Iliff in Arizona, Rosey Cameron-Smith in St Kitts, Marcia de Castro and Augusta Leite Campos in Brazil, and Bianca Botta, fresh from the White Mountains in California.

It has been my happy experience that the staff of libraries and other centres of research are always prepared to go that little bit further in their efforts to help. I continue to thank you all, particularly the

THE AFRICAN BAOBAB

researchers in the East African Natural History Society, knowing that your efforts were made no easier by my technophobia.

Leaving the libraries and moving on to publishers – no one could hope for a better relationship with their publisher than I have had with Pippa Parker, who has put so much faith in my writing efforts since she read the first draft of the first edition. Nor could I ever expect to have an easier relationship with an editor than I do with charming Natalie Bell. Emily Vosloo has been a wonderful designer too. Thank you Emily.

Much of my travel around baobabs was undertaken in the company of my wife, Mary Ann, who senses things in trees I never do, and has used their healing properties in her work. We have marvelled at hundreds of baobab trees together, and I know there are hundreds more awaiting our attentions.

Not only in Africa, but also in Madagascar, some baobab trees have scars showing where panels of bark have been stripped off the trunk.

Selected bibliography

The first edition of this book contains a detailed bibliography, including in particular sources not easily found on the internet. The second edition continues to owe a debt to almost all of these, but rather than mention them again, I repeat my thanks for other people's efforts and set out below both a few of the especially helpful sources from the first bibliography and then some of those that have contributed to the revisions of the text in this second edition.

The best general overview of the African baobab and its family ...

Was formerly found in a paper by Wickens, G E, **The Baobab – Africa's Upside Down Tree**, in *Kew Bulletin*, Vol. 37(2), 1982, but this has been far surpassed by that writer's incredible compendium of 'baobabilia', written in collaboration with Pat Lowe, *The Baobabs: Pachycauls of Africa, Madagascar and Australia*, published by Springer Nature, Dordrecht, 2008.

Taxonomy has received its share of attention over the past decade.

David Baum probably knows more about baobabs than anyone else on Earth. Any paper to which he puts his name deserves attention and his 1995 paper, **A systematic revision of *Adansonia* (Bombacaceae)**, published in *Annals of the Missouri Botanical Garden* Vol. 82, remains as relevant today as it was then. Latterly, an attempt was made by Pettigrew J D and others to split *Adansonia digitata* into two distinct species in their 2012 paper, **Morphology, ploidy and molecular phylogenetics reveal a new diploid species from Africa in the baobab genus *Adansonia* (Malvaceae: Bombacoideae)**, published in *Taxon*, Vol. 61(6). This view was refuted four years later in Vol. 65(5) of the same journal by Cron G V and others, including David Baum, in **One African baobab species or two? Synonymy of *Adansonia kilima* and *A. digitata***.

Further researches into the biology of the African species continue.

Karimi N and others (again including David Baum) advanced the role of hawkmoths in pollinating baobabs in **Evidence for hawkmoth pollination in the chiropterophilous African baobab *(Adansonia digitata)***, published in *Biotropica*, December 2021. Another recent study goes some way to explaining why some trees fruit profusely year after year, and others hardly at all; Chetty A et al published **Reproductive ecology of the African baobab: Floral features differ among individuals with different fruit production**, in *Forest Ecology and Management*, Vol. 489, 2021.

Efforts to date baobabs are fortunately never going to stop.

Working out of Babes-Bolyai University in Romania, professor Adrian Patrut has established a reputation as the doyen of carbon-dating baobab trees. Of his many papers on the subject, always written in conjunction with others, **The demise of the largest and oldest African baobabs**, appearing in *Nature Plants*, Vol. 4, 2018 is a particularly helpful and readable summary of the state and estimated age of the big, old trees in southern Africa. Other papers on which I have drawn include **Radiocarbon dating of a very large African baobab (the Grootboom in Namibia)**, published in *Tree Physiology*, Vol. 27(11), 2007, and **Age, Growth and Death of a National Icon: The Historic Chapman Baobab of Botswana**, appearing in *Forests*, Vol. 10, 2019.

The state of African baobabs in India has also received attention ...

again by A Patrut et al in **Radiocarbon dating of two old African baobabs from India**, *PLOS* 2020, and by Singh, R K in *Plight of the oldest baobab (Adansonia digitata L.) tree of India at Jhunsi, Allahabad,* published by Indian Forester, 2017.

THE AFRICAN BAOBAB

... while interest in other baobab species is as strong as ever.

S Andriantsaralaza discussed *Frugivory and seed dispersal of endemic Malagasy baobabs after Megafauna extinction* at the 2019 Island Biology Conference in La Réunion, while news station ABC Kimberley in Australia featured a discussion in radio show 'Curious Kimberley' on 7 August 2018: *Scientists disagree how boab trees got to Australia from Africa and Madagascar*.

With the soaring demand for baobab products, research is now being undertaken on domesticating the trees.

Several articles on this topic enlightened me. Gurashi, N A et al's **Ethnobotany of Wild Baobab *(Adansonia digitata L.)*: A Way Forward for Species Domestication and Conservation in Sudan**, was published in *Journal of Forest and Environmental Science*, Vol. 33(4), 2017. Agbohessou M et al wrote **Status of vegetative propagation of baobabs; a review**, in *African Crop Science Journal*, Vol. 28, 2020. More recently Egbadzor, K F & Akuaku, J wrote optimistically about **Prospects of raising baobab *(Adansonia digitata L.)* to fruiting in two years**, in *Trees, Forests and People*, Vol. 8, 2022.

The long-term future for baobabs is sadly depressing.

This was studied by Venter, S M & Witowski, E T F in **Where are the young baobabs? Factors affecting regeneration of *Adansonia digitata L.* in a communally managed area of southern Africa**, published in *Journal of Arid Environments*, Vol. 92, 2013, while linking growth to climate was the paper from my correspondent Diana H Mayne and others: **Baobabs at the edge; 90-year dynamics of climate variability, growth, resilience, and evolutionary legacy effects**, in *Frontiers in Forests and Global Change*, November 2022.

Many thanks to the writers of all the above papers, and to the many other authors whose works I have consulted but failed to acknowledge.

A perfect, peaceful resting place at the end of the day.

Photographic credits

All the images in this book are copyright © Rupert Watson, with the exception of the following individual photographers and institutions. **AS** = stock.adobe.com, **WC** = via Wikimedia Commons

Front cover: hannesthirion – AS
Half-title page: Diversity Studio – AS
Title page: Roger de la Harpe – AS
6: Sarah Venter
12: Pascal06 – AS
13 right: Dordo – AS
14–15: Picturellarious – AS
16: 169169 – AS
17: Diana Mayne
19: s-aznar – AS
21: Gallica, Public domain, WC
22: Hunt Institute for Botanical Documentation
23: Thomas Baines (1820–1875), Public domain, WC
33: Mirabelle – AS
37: Barth, Heinrich, 1821–1865, No restrictions, WC
40–41: 9elisa9 – AS
42: Oscar Espinosa – AS
43: Marcia de Castro and Augusta Leite Campos
44: Nick86174|Dreamstime.com
45: Miller, Philip. *Gardeners Dictionary*. London: Law & Gilbert for F.C. & J. Rivington, etc, 1731. Internet Archive
46–47: drimafilm – AS
48–49: ogurisu – AS
50: Marco Schmidt, CC BY-SA 3.0, WC

52–53: Roger de la Harpe – AS
57: Susie Allan
58: merlintuttle.org
62 top: Biodiversity Heritage Library, Public domain; **bottom right:** ArtushFoto – AS
66–67: Filippo – AS
69: forcdan – AS
71: Estate of Antoine de Saint-Exupéry
74: Kathryn – AS
76 left: Al Carrera – AS
77: Royal Geographical Society (with IBG)
80–81: ChrisOvergaard – AS
82 top: michelealfieri – AS
84 top: hakoar – AS
86: Hans – AS
87: gi0572 – AS
99: Grantat – AS
100: John Theodor – AS
102–3: www.dariomirelli.com – AS
105: Fearless on 4 Wheels – AS
108: Bianca Botta
109: konoplizkaya – AS
110: Royal Geographical Society (with IBG)
111: Chris – AS
113: Quentin and Simon Keynes
114: Amritanshu Tripathi, CC BY-SA 4.0, WC

117: Carol Beckwith
119: Gary – AS
126–7: rufar – AS
135 left: Ian White
136: dhvstockphoto – AS
138–9: Александр Катаржин – AS
141: lucaar – AS
143: Carol Beckwith
144: Philippe Prudhomme – AS
148–9: tolly65 – AS
152: Mannaggia – AS
154–5: EinBlick – AS
156: compuinfoto – AS
157: jean claude braun – AS
159: GL Archive / Alamy / AfriPics
163: julianwphoto – AS
165: Nattapol_Sritongcom – AS
168: august.columbo – AS
171: Sergey – AS
173: Reto Ammann – AS
182–3: hannesthirion – AS
184–5: Александр Катаржин – AS
186 top: Dr Hugh Bunting
191: lunamarina – AS
193: Vince Shaft – AS
196–7: crazycolors – AS
205: ileiry – AS
207: BotswanaPost
Back cover, author photo: Mary Ann Burris
Spine: Maria.Epine – AS

Botswana celebrates its botanical heritage on its postage stamps, these ones all depicting baobab trees.

THE AFRICAN BAOBAB